Partnership Working to Support Special Educational Needs and Disabilities

SAGE has been part of the global academic community
since 1965, supporting high quality research and learning
that transforms society and our understanding of individuals,
groups, and cultures. SAGE is the independent, innovative,
natural home for authors, editors and societies who share
our commitment and passion for the social sciences.

Find out more at: **www.sagepublications.com**

Partnership Working to Support Special Educational Needs and Disabilities

Rona Tutt

Los Angeles | London | New Delhi
Singapore | Washington DC

First published 2011

Apart from any fair dealing for the purposes of research or
private study, or criticism or review, as permitted under
the Copyright, Designs and Patents Act, 1988, this
publication may be reproduced, stored or transmitted in
any form, or by any means, only with the prior permission
in writing of the publishers, or in the case of reprographic
reproduction, in accordance with the terms of licences
issued by the Copyright Licensing Agency. Enquiries
concerning reproduction outside those terms should be
sent to the publishers.

SAGE Publications Ltd
1 Oliver's Yard
55 City Road
London EC1Y 1SP

SAGE Publications Inc.
2455 Teller Road
Thousand Oaks, California 91320

SAGE Publications India Pvt Ltd
B 1/I 1 Mohan Cooperative Industrial Area
Mathura Road
New Delhi 110 044

SAGE Publications Asia-Pacific Pte Ltd
33 Pekin Street #02-01
Far East Square
Singapore 048763

Library of Congress Control Number: 2010924776

British Library Cataloguing in Publication data

A catalogue record for this book is available from the British Library

ISBN 978-0-85702-147-2
ISBN 978-0-85702-148-9 (pbk)

Typeset by C&M Digitals (P) Ltd, Chennai, India
Printed in Great Britain by CPI Antony Rowe, Chippenham, Wiltshire
Printed on paper from sustainable resources

Dedication

This book is dedicated to those who strive to find innovative approaches to enhance the educational opportunities for children and young people who have special educational needs and disabilities (SEND).

About the author

Dr Rona Tutt OBE has taught children with SEN and disabilities in state and independent, residential and day, mainstream and special schools. Trained originally as a teacher of deaf children, she became the head teacher of Woolgrove School in Hertfordshire, a school for pupils who have moderate learning difficulties (MLD). She established the local authority's first provision for pupils on the autism spectrum within the school. In 2003, Rona was the winner of the Leadership in Teaching Award. In 2004, she received an OBE for her services to special needs education. From 2004 to 2005, she was President of the National Association of Head Teachers (NAHT). She continues to work for them as a SEN consultant.

Rona writes on a number of educational issues and is much in demand as a speaker. In 2007, her first book, *Every Child Included*, was published. The book looked beyond the inclusion debate to illustrate, by means of case studies of schools and other settings, the range of provision that is developing. At the same time, she considered how schools are addressing the Every Child Matters agenda alongside their provision for SEN.

In 2008, she co-authored a second book with the cognitive neuropsychologist, Winand H. Dittrich, *Educating Children with Complex Conditions – Understanding Overlapping and Co-existing Disorders*. This book brings together some of the latest research on how the brain works with what is known about a group of neurodevelopmental disorders: ADHD, autism, specific language impairment and the specific learning difficulties of dyslexia, dyscalculia, dyspraxia and dysgraphia. It provides practical guidance for school leaders and practitioners on how to use this knowledge to provide for children and young people who have complex conditions.

Rona has an MA in Linguistics and a PhD in the education of pupils with autism. She is Chair of Governors at Heathlands School in St Albans, which caters for severely and profoundly deaf children, and Vice Chair of Governors at The Valley School in Stevenage, which is for secondary pupils with MLD, autism and other complex needs.

Contents

Acknowledgements

I would like to offer my sincere thanks to the leaders of the schools, services and settings who allowed me to highlight their work in the case studies and who generously gave me their time when I visited. These include:

Barrs Court School
Corbets Tey School
Dacorum Education Support Centre
Darlington Education Village
Disability Inclusion Service, Warwickshire
Furze Down School
Goddard Park Primary School
Grangewood School
Greys Education Centre
Hounslow Town Primary School
Le Murier School
Le Rondin School and Centre
Nottingham Regional Society for Adults and Children with Autism (NORSACA)
St Piers School
St Sampson's High School
St Vincent's School
Shaftesbury High School
Shiremoor Primary School
South Dartmoor Community College
The Hereford Academy
The St Christopher School
The St Marylebone School
Woodlands High School

I am indebted to:

Members of NAHT's Special Educational Needs and Disability Committee, for their encouragement and support;
Wendy Skyte and her colleagues at the Specialist Schools and Academies Trust (SSAT) for giving me an introduction to schools;
Tricia Murphy, former President of Nasen, and many colleagues who allowed me to use them as a sounding board, while putting up with my neglect of them;
My husband David for his practical assistance in overcoming any technical problems and keeping the household under control, while I was otherwise engaged,
And, finally, to Jude Bowen, Senior Commissioning Editor and Amy Jarrold, Assistant Editor at Sage, for their patience when publication was delayed by recurring and substantial snowfalls.

How to use this book

This book explains ways in which schools are finding new ways of providing more effectively for children and young people who have special educational needs and disabilities (SEND). Each of the main chapters illustrates different ways in which partnership working is leading to a richer experience for pupils who, for a variety of very different reasons, find it hard to learn.

Although readers may prefer to dip into the book as they choose, it may be helpful to bear in mind how the chapters are arranged:

The introductory chapter sets the scene by considering both the changing structures of schools and how children's needs are changing.

Chapter 1 looks at the key relationship between learners and those who guide their learning, and at the importance of involving young people and their families in the education process.

Chapter 2 focuses on how individual schools are forming partnerships with other schools through outreach work and through becoming specialist schools with a SEN specialism.

Chapter 3 moves on from the work that individual schools initiate, to consider how groups of schools are collaborating through being co-located, federated or working in partnership in other ways, including developing relationships with short stay schools (formerly known as pupil referral units).

Chapter 4 examines how schools are looking outwards and developing wider partnerships through becoming academies, trust schools, or setting up other business links.

Chapter 5 concentrates on interagency working, from the perspective of children's centres, extended schools and services for children and young people with SEND.

Chapter 6 is in a different style and is designed as a resource. It has photocopiable materials that readers can use to stimulate discussion or as a starting point for developing their own strategies.

The concluding chapter brings together the themes that have been running through the book and draws some conclusions about the value of partnership working and how collaboration is likely to become even more crucial in supporting children and young people with increasingly complex needs.

Chapters 1–5 have a similar format:

- The main points of the chapter are outlined at the start.
- 'Key points' are highlighted throughout the chapter and, for ease of reference, also appear in the glossary at the back of the book.
- 'Questions for reflection' are raised at relevant points in each chapter, to encourage the reader to interact with the text and to provide a basis for wider debate and discussion.

- 'Case studies' of schools and services are used to demonstrate ways in which the changing structures of schools and services benefit children and young people with SEND.
- The chapters end with a summary of what has been covered, followed by suggestions for further reading.

I hope the book will convey something of the dynamism and innovation I found when visiting the schools in the case studies. In today's pressured climate, it is all too easy to be overwhelmed by the rapidity and extent of change, but sometimes it is possible to seize the opportunities that these developments bring and to use them to enrich the educational experiences of those for whom learning presents a challenge. This is what the schools and settings in the case studies, and many like them, have set out to do.

Abbreviations and acronyms

ADD	Attention deficit disorder
ADHD	Attention deficit hyperactivity disorder
AEN	Additional educational needs
ALN	Additional learning needs
ASDAN	Award Scheme Development and Accreditation Network
AST	Advanced skills teacher
BESD	Behaviour, emotional and social difficulties
BSF	Building Schools for the Future
CAB	Citizens Advice Bureau
CAMHS	Child and Adolescent Mental Health Services
CATS	Consortium of all-through schooling
CCEA	Council for the Curriculum, Examinations and Assessment (N. Ireland)
CCTA	City College of Technology and the Arts
CDC	Child Development Centre
CEO	Chief Education Officer
CLDD	Complex learning difficulties and disabilities
CoPE	Certificate of Personal Effectiveness
CPD	Continuing Professional Development
CSP	Commissioning Support Programme
CTC	City Technology College
DCELLS	Department for Children, Education, Lifelong Learning and Skills (Wales)
DCSF	Department for Children, Schools and Families
DESC	Dacorum Education Support Centre
DfE	Department for Education
DfES	Department for Education and Skills
EAL	English as an additional language
ECM	Every Child Matters
EDI	Education and Development International
EEC	Early Excellence Centre
EP	Educational Psychologist
EPS	Educational Psychology Service
ESRA	Extended schools remodelling adviser
ET	Excellent teacher
EWO	Education Welfare Officer
FASD	Foetal alcohol syndrome disorder
FE	Further education
GCSE	General Certificate of Secondary Education
GM	Grant maintained
GTP	Graduate teacher programme
HE	Higher education

HLTA	Higher level teaching assistant
HPSS	High performing specialist school
LA	Local authority
LEA	Local education authority
LLDD	Learners with learning difficulties and disabilities
LSC	Learning and Skills Council
LSW	Learning support workers
MLD	Moderate learning difficulties
MSAs	Midday supervisory assistants
MSI	Multisensory impairment
Nasen	National Association of Special Education Needs
NCEE	National Council for Educational Excellence
NCYPE	National Centre for Young People with Epilepsy
NEET	Not in education, employment or training
NORSACA	Nottingham Regional Society for Adults and Children with Autism
NPQICL	National Professional Qualification in Integrated Centre Leadership
Ofqual	Office of Qualifications and Examinations Regulation
OSHL	Out of school hours learning
PCP	Primary Capital Programme
PCT	Primary Care Trust
PFA	Parents and Friends Association
PFI	Private Finance Initiative
PLTS	Personal, learning and thinking skills
PMLD	Profound and multiple learning difficulties
PPP	Public–private partnerships
PPS	Parent Partnership Services
PRU	Pupil referral unit
PSA	Parent support adviser
PTA	Parent Teacher Association
QTS	Qualified teacher status
RNIB	Royal National Institute for the Blind
RRSA	Rights Respecting School Award
SaLT	Speech and language therapist
SCQF	Scottish Credit and Qualifications Framework
SEN	Special educational needs
SEND	Special educational needs and disabilities
SFA	Skills funding agency
SLCN	Speech, language and communication needs
SLD	Severe learning difficulties
SLI	Specific language impairment
SSAT	Specialist Schools and Academies Trust
SST	Specialist Schools Trust
TA	Teaching assistant
TDA	Training and development agency (for schools)
TVEI	Technical and Vocational Education Initiative
UN	United Nations
UNCRC	UN Convention on the Rights of the Child

VA   Voluntary aided (schools)
VC   Voluntary controlled (schools)
VLE   Virtual learning environment
YPLA   Young People's Learning Agency

Introduction

This introduction sets the scene for the rest of the book by outlining:

- ways in which schools and other educational settings are becoming more diverse
- how these changes are leading to schools working in partnership and taking shared responsibility for children and young people, including those with special educational needs and disabilities (SEND)
- the increasing expectations of what schools will provide and their role within the community
- how the changing needs of children and young people, and the way they are described, needs to be borne in mind alongside these other changes.

How schools are changing

The last two decades have seen an unprecedented growth in the diversity of schools that have been created. In addition, schools have taken on new roles and responsibilities. Some of these changes can be summarised as follows:

- children and young people being encouraged to be active participants in the learning process
- parents and carers being seen as partners in their children's education
- schools becoming more varied in terms of how they operate
- educational settings engaging with a range of outside bodies
- the expectation that education, health and social care will work closely together.

This book explains some of these changes and provides examples of how a variety of schools, settings and services have used the opportunities created by new ways of working to provide more effectively for children and young people who have special educational needs and disabilities (SEND). The common thread linking these changes has been the move to schools working in partnership, both with each other and with other agencies.

The journey to greater diversity

There have been many attempts to change the structure and status of schools. Although some of these have been mainly to do with secondary schools, all

1

have had an effect on the primary phase as well. The 1944 Education Act (sometimes referred to after its originator, R.A. Butler, as the Butler Act) was the one that made secondary education available to all pupils, apart from those who, because of their limited intellectual capacity, were considered to be *ineducable*. (A similar Act was introduced in Scotland in 1945.) The Act proposed a tripartite system of education, with the most academically able who passed the 11+ examination going to a grammar school and those who did not pass being sent either to a technical school or to a secondary modern school. As very few technical schools were built and only a minority of pupils passed the 11+, this left the majority of pupils starting their secondary education with a sense of failure. This situation continued until the 1970s, when comprehensive education largely replaced the idea of dividing pupils according to their academic ability and students of all abilities (apart from those who were in the remaining grammar schools or in special schools) began to be educated together. Today, there are still a few parts of the country where children sit the 11+ and, despite many efforts to dismantle them, 164 grammar schools remain.

Specialist schools

The argument about whether or not it is right to admit pupils according to their ability came back to some degree in the 1990s, when the government introduced the idea of specialist schools. These schools are able to admit up to 10% of pupils on their aptitude for the subject in which the school specialises, although very few have chosen to do so.

 Key points: Specialist schools

- The Specialist Schools Programme began in 1994, with the aim of enabling secondary schools to become centres of excellence in their chosen specialism.
- Specialist schools receive additional funding and as well as raising standards in their own schools, they are expected to establish partnerships with other schools, so that expertise and experience can be shared.
- Specialist schools have the option of calling themselves colleges rather than schools and many have chosen to do so.
- The programme is also open to special schools that have secondary-aged pupils.

The creation of specialist schools was a significant step towards encouraging schools to work together and to share responsibility for the progress of their pupils. This is in contrast to previous years, when competition between schools was seen by government as the key to raising standards. (Further information and case studies of specialist schools appear in Chapter 2).

Questions for reflection

1. What do you see as the advantages and disadvantages of some schools catering for more academically able pupils?
2. Do you think there is a clear distinction between ability and aptitude? If so, how would you define the difference?
3. Does this distinction hold true for all subjects? For instance, is it easier to recognise an aptitude for sport or the arts, than an aptitude for maths?

Not long after the Specialist Schools Programme had become established, the next major addition to new types of schools were the academies, which came into being at the turn of the century. Originally known as *City Academies*, the word *city* was dropped so that academies could be established in rural areas as well as inner cities.

Academies

The original aim of the academies programme was to drive up standards by replacing schools that were seen as 'failing' in terms of their low examination results, with a new breed of schools that have greater autonomy. Often situated in areas of deprivation, these academies occupy new buildings (or move into them as soon as possible after becoming academies), whose architecture is often far removed from the traditional secondary school. The modern buildings and additional resources, both in terms of funding and support from outside sponsors, are seen as giving pupils from disadvantaged backgrounds, greater opportunity to engage with learning.

 Key points: Academies and independent schools

Academies are described as state-maintained independent schools, which seems a contradiction in terms, but they are independent in the sense that they are funded directly from Whitehall, rather than by the local authority (LA) in which they are situated. Academies are supported by sponsors.

Independent Schools are sometimes referred to as private schools, or, confusingly, as public schools. They are independent of the state and funded by fees from parents. There are about 2300 independent schools and about 250 of these are special schools. Independent and non-maintained special schools (the latter having fees paid by LAs rather than parents) often cater for pupils at the most complex end of the SEND continuum.

Most academies have been secondary schools, although the number of all-through academies has increased. In May 2010, an Academies Bill was introduced by the Coalition Government, to enable primary and special schools to become academies. (Examples of academies, and further information about them, is given in Chapter 4.)

Trust schools

After the emergence of specialist schools in 1994 and academies in 2000, a further development in the diversification of schools was the creation of trust schools. These were signalled in the white paper, *Higher Standards, Better Schools for All* (DfES, 2005a). A school has to be a foundation school (which was an option some schools took up under the 1998 Act), before becoming a trust school.

⚷ Key points: Foundation status and trust schools

Under the Standards and Framework Act (1998), there were three categories of maintained schools:

1. Community schools – these are run by the LA, which employs the staff, owns the buildings and land, and decides on the arrangements for admitting pupils.
2. Voluntary controlled (VC)/voluntary aided (VA) schools – these are generally church schools and the relevant church shares some of the responsibilities with the LA.
3. Foundation schools – in common with VC and VA schools, these schools have a greater involvement in how they are run. The land and buildings may be owned by the governing body or by a charitable trust.
4. Trust schools did not exist at the time of the 1998 Act, but came about as the result of the 2006 Education and Inspections Act (DfES, 2006a). They are foundation schools which are supported by a charitable foundation or 'trust'.

A trust may consist of one school or a group of schools. Primary, secondary and special schools can all become trust schools. (Additional information about trust schools is given in Chapter 4, together with some examples).

Although specialist schools, academies and trust schools have been described separately, a school may fit more than one of these descriptions. For instance, specialist schools may become trust schools and academies are able to develop specialisms. All three types of schools have taken forward the idea of working with a range of partners. The white paper *Your Child, Your Schools, Our Future: Building a 21st Century School System* (DCSF, 2009c) sees partnership arrangements, including federations, as being central to the education system of the future. (Federated schools and co-located schools and services are described in Chapter 3).

Changing expectations of schools

Although there are many different types of schools now in existence, they are all concerned with the idea of partnership working in one way or another. While the majority of schools have always preferred to work collaboratively rather than to be in competition with each other, the atmosphere created by the standards agenda, with its emphasis on judging schools very publicly on a narrow range of outcomes, has not been conducive to partnership working, particularly as schools have such very different intakes and challenges. Being judged in this way has also discouraged schools from welcoming pupils with SEND, as they are more likely to have a negative impact on the school's performance.

While a strong element of competition remains, collaboration between schools is being encouraged through the new structures that have been mentioned, as well as through the formation of a number of partnerships between groups of schools. These have become necessary as no school on its own can cover everything it is expected to do, from becoming an extended school, to secondary schools needing to give their students access to the full range of options from 14–19. One of the most crucial links, particularly for children and young people with SEND, has been the joining up of the education service with health and social care.

The effects of ECM and the Children Act (2004)

The changing expectations of what schools will provide have stemmed from the Green Paper *Every Child Matters* (ECM) (DfES, 2003) and the Children Act (DfES, 2004a) that followed it. The effect on schools of the ECM agenda has to be set in the context of what the Act has meant at national and local level. This has changed the face of the whole education system. After the Act, the former Department for Education and Skills (DfES) became the Department for Children, Schools and Families (DCSF). The title of Secretary of State for Education disappeared and was replaced by the Secretary of State for Children, Schools and Families. Local education authorities (LEAs) as separate entities became subsumed within a local authority's (LA's) children's services department, mirroring the demise of the DfES. As a consequence, Directors of Education or Chief Education Officers (CEOs) were replaced by Directors of Children's Services. In May 2010, the Coalition Government changed the name of the Department back to the Department for Education (DfE).

Extended schools

The expectations of schools in The Children Act were underlined by the government's ten-year strategy, *The Children's Plan: Building Brighter Futures* (DCSF, 2007). This confirmed that by 2010, all schools would be expected to provide access to a range of extended services. The word 'access' is important, as it means that individual schools will vary in terms of what each will provide. Not every school has the capacity to develop a full range of services, but every school can make a contribution, as well as signposting to where other activities are available.

Children's centres

Children's centres offer early education and childcare, as well as wider family support and access to health services on a single site, although exactly how much a particular children's centre offers depends on the needs of the neighbourhood where it is located. (Case studies of extended schools and children's centres are provided in Chapter 5).

There is no doubt that the extended schools agenda has put extra pressure on schools, which some may see as detracting from their core purpose of educating pupils. Others view it as a way of raising standards, because of the wider approach it offers to supporting children's learning from an early age, together with that of their families. What is certain is that schools have become radically different institutions from those that existed even ten or twenty years ago.

 Questions for reflection

1. What do you see as the positive side of having a number of different types of schools?
2. Do you think there are negatives as well?
3. In your opinion, are extended schools in danger of losing their focus on improving teaching and learning, or do they add a new dimension to it?
4. What do you see as the benefits of children's centres and extended schools for children with SEND?

The changing needs of children and young people

So far, this chapter has considered how schools are changing in terms of the variety of schools that exist and the roles they are expected to play. Alongside these changes, the nature of children's needs, and how they are described, is constantly changing too.

Terminology

The term special educational needs (SEN) originated from the Warnock Report of 1978 and the subsequent Education Act of 1981. It is a much broader term than 'handicapped' which was the term used pre-Warnock. Indeed, the full title of the Warnock Report was the *Report of the Committee of Enquiry into the Education of Handicapped Children and Young People.* Warnock used the umbrella term *SEN* to focus on the needs of children as individuals rather than thinking of them in terms of categories of need, such as maladjusted or educationally sub-normal (two of the terms in use at the time). It was also to recognise a much larger group of children than the 2% who, at that time, were educated in special schools.

SEN and disability

Over time, the term 'disability', which is used by the health service, has broadened as well. At one time, it was used mainly to describe those who had a physical disability, but it now covers a wide range of disabilities. In 2001, SEN and disability were brought together in the SEN and Disability

Act (often referred to as 'SENDA') (DfES, 2001a). Although the two terms are not synonymous, there is now a large degree of overlap and the acronym *SEND* has come into use. In Scotland, the term *additional educational needs* (AEN) is used to cover SEND and other vulnerable groups, such as looked after children, the disaffected and those at risk of exclusion. Sometimes the term AEN or additional learning needs (ALN) is used in England, and, when it is, it generally encompasses this wider group as well as SEND.

Changing descriptions within SEND

Although Warnock wanted to shift the focus away from categorising children to concentrating on their needs as individuals, 30 years after the work of the Warnock Committee, an increasing number of labels is being used. Partly this is a result of better diagnosis and partly it is because new needs are being recognised. Improved diagnosis means that, for instance, children on the autism spectrum are given that label rather than being seen as having communication or behavioural difficulties; attention deficit hyperactivity disorder (ADHD) is treated as a separate diagnosis within behaviour, emotional and social difficulties (BESD), and dyslexia is no longer used synonymously with specific learning difficulties (SpLD), because dyscalculia, dyspraxia and dysgraphia are recognised as well.

A second reason for an increase in labels is the appearance of new disorders. These include new and rare chromosomal disorders which are being identified, as well as needs that are arising from premature babies surviving after being born increasingly early. Some of these babies will have conditions such as foetal alcohol syndrome disorder (FASD). The incidence of FASD is said to be as high as that of autism (roughly one in a hundred) and it is another condition that was rarely mentioned until comparatively recently. As it is caused by the mother's drinking affecting the development of the baby's brain while in the womb, unlike most conditions, FASD is entirely preventable.

The combination of better diagnosis plus the emergence of new conditions, means that there has also been a marked increase in children and young people being assessed or diagnosed as having co-existing conditions, such as autism and ADHD, or dyslexia, dyspraxia and a specific language impairment (SLI).

Addressing changing needs

What this means is that all types of schools are on the receiving end of children with more complex needs, whether that complexity is caused by the severity of their learning difficulty or by having a combination of conditions. With a reduction in special school places and the trend ever since Warnock to include pupils in their local schools, mainstream schools are seeing pupils who would previously have been in special schools, while special schools have moved from catering for specific needs to having a much more diverse and complex population. Pupils who have moderate learning difficulties (MLD), for instance, are no longer to be found in specialist provision, unless they have other needs as well.

There is also a heightened awareness and interest in SEND. More information has been put in the public domain since the Special Educational Needs (SEN) Information Act was passed in 2008 (DCSF, 2008d). This means that the government annually has to publish information on children with SEN which includes:

- the characteristics of children with SEN
- their attainment levels
- their absences and exclusions from school
- the views of pupils with a learning difficulty from the Tellus 3 survey.

(There is further information on the Tellus surveys in the next chapter).

In the last few years, there has been an unusually large number of reviews, reports and inquiries focusing on SEND, including: Sir Alan Steer's work on behaviour (DfES, 2005b and DCSF, 2009b); a review of CAMHS, the child and adolescent mental health service (DCSF and DoH, 2008a); John Bercow's review of services for speech, language and communication needs (SLCN) (DCSF, 2008b); Sir Jim Rose's report on the teaching of children with dyslexia (2009g); Brian Lamb's inquiry into increasing parental confidence in the SEN system (DCSF, 2009h) and the current Ofsted SEN Survey, 2009/10. These demonstrate the growing interest in how to help pupils with SEND, and will be referred to in subsequent chapters.

As no school on its own can be expected to meet the needs of every child in an era when learning is expected to be more personalised to the individual, and, at the same time, children's needs are becoming more complex, it is encouraging that, regardless of the type of provision, partnership working is coming to the fore and, with it, fresh opportunities to draw on a wider range of expertise and experience that may benefit children and young people who have SEND.

☐ Summary

This chapter has considered some of the many ways in which schools are changing, both in terms of the diversity of schools that now exist, the expectations of what schools will provide, and the move towards working in partnership, both with each other and with a broad range of other services and organisations.

Consideration has also been given to the changing terminology around SEND and the growing complexity presented by children and young people, whether in mainstream or specialist provision, which highlights the importance of schools and services working collaboratively, so that expertise can be shared and additional opportunities presented to those for whom learning does not come easily.

Further reading

Department for Children, Schools and Families (2009) *Your Child, Your Schools, Our Future: Building a 21st Century School System.* Available at www.dcsf.gov.uk/21stcenturyschoolssystem

Dittrich, W.H. and Tutt, R. (2008) *Educating Children with Complex Conditions: Understanding Overlapping and Co-existing Developmental Disorders.* London: Sage.

Hill, R. (2008) *Achieving More Together: Adding Value Through Partnership.* Leicester: Association of School and College Leaders.

Todd, L. (2007) *Partnerships for Inclusive Education.* London: Routledge.

1

Working in partnership with pupils and parents

> **This chapter considers:**
>
> - the move towards making learning more personalised
> - the increasing importance of listening to the voice of pupils and involving them as active participants in learning
> - the growing appreciation of what can be achieved by schools and families working in partnership.
>
> These three elements: personalising learning, pupil voice and parental involvement, are examined in relation to their significance for pupils for whom learning involves particular challenges.

The previous chapter looked at some of the ways in which schools are changing, in terms of their growing diversity, the move to schools working collaboratively with each other, and the expectation that schools will combine with other services and organisations to become the centre of their communities. Alongside these developments, the changing needs of children and young people were touched on, too. Before moving on in subsequent chapters to look at how partnership working is evolving in different educational settings, this chapter considers the fundamental relationship between staff and pupils, and between schools and families.

Pupils as Partners in Learning

Learning in school is no longer viewed as an experience where teachers are the active participants in the process and pupils the passive recipients. The students of today expect to be given a degree of choice as to what they study and how they learn. This reflects a general trend in society, from professionals deciding on the services clients should receive, to people being consulted about the services they want and how they would like them to be provided. In education, this movement gathered momentum when the idea of personalised learning was first introduced.

Personalising learning

In 2004, when David Miliband was Minister of State for School Standards, he gave a speech in which he described how personalised learning might become the defining feature of the education system. He described it as providing an education to every child, 'which is tailored to their unique learning styles, motivations and needs'. This was published as a pamphlet by the DfES (2005) and the above quote appears in the Foreword. Two years later, Christine Gilbert (before becoming Her Majesty's Chief Inspector of Schools) was asked to lead a government review into what the personalisation of teaching and learning might look like. In her report, *2020 Vision: Report of the Teaching and Learning in 2020 Review Group* (DfES, 2006b), Gilbert confirmed that personalised learning has a central role to play in transforming the education service in England. The report went on to say that the link between learning and teaching is strengthened if pupils and parents are seen as partners in the process.

When the idea of personalising learning first came to the fore, it was greeted with some degree of scepticism. There were understandable concerns that it would involve trying to provide an individual curriculum for every pupil. As the understanding grew of what was involved, the fears diminished. For many years, educationalists have been interested in Gardner's (2000) idea of recognising several types of intelligence, as well as the notion that people have different learning styles. Both of these ideas led to a greater awareness of the need to treat children and young people as individuals who have their own interests, abilities and characteristics. Every child matters, as the Green Paper of that title pointed out, and every child should matter equally, so that learning is tailored to individual needs. It has been accepted that pupils who have special educational needs and disabilities (SEND) may require a more individualised approach because of the nature of their learning difficulties. Personalising learning for every pupil is a step on from this. Indeed, it is conceivable that, if personalised learning for all really takes root, there would not need to be a separate category for pupils with SEND, as all pupils would have their needs met in the most appropriate way. This in no way suggests that every type of help, including learning at a different pace, benefiting from the support of therapists or having specialist equipment, would no longer be available, but that there would be no need to single out pupils with SEND in the way that it is done at the moment.

There are very close links between personalising a pupil's learning experiences and listening to the voice of the child. The more students' voices are heard, the more likely it is that a curriculum can be delivered in a way that meets their needs and encourages them to take an active interest in their learning, both now and in the future. With the pace of change in all areas of life, it is essential that school is seen as the beginning of a person's education and that learning is accepted as being a lifelong activity.

The rise of 'Pupil Voice'

There has been a gradual shift over many years to recognising the importance of listening to the views of children. The growing interest in pupil voice is demonstrated by the rise in the number of student councils across primary, secondary and special schools, as well as other ways in which the voice of the child is being given increasing importance. In educational terms, a child's perspective brings another dimension to teaching and learning, shedding fresh light on the learning process and helping pupils to be motivated by feeling part of that process.

United Nations Convention on the Rights of the Child (UNCRC)

The trend towards taking more note of children's views was given impetus by the United Nations Convention on the Rights of the Child (UNCRC), which was ratified in 1989 and came into force in England in 1992. This is an international treaty for children's rights, which has been agreed by almost all the UN member states. UNCRC gives children and young people a specific right to be heard and to be listened to.

 Key points: UN Convention on the Rights of the Child (UNCRC)

UNCRC has 54 articles that give young people up to the age of 18 specific rights. The key provisions are:

- the right to a childhood protected from harm
- the right to an education
- the right to be healthy
- the right to be treated fairly
- the right to be heard.

UNICEF's *Little Book of Children's Rights and Responsibilities* (2007) contains a summary of the articles in UNCRC.

Some of these rights are similar to the five outcomes of ECM. They are also reflected in the DCSF's (2007) *The Children's Plan: Building Brighter Futures;* in the Scottish Government's approach *Getting it right for every child* (2006); Northern Ireland's *Our Children and Young People – Our Pledge: a Ten Year Strategy for Children and Young People* (Office of the First Minister and Deputy First Minister, 2006); and in the approach of the Welsh Assembly Government, where its work with children and young people is structured around seven core aims based on UNCRC.

Every five years, the UK Government has to report on its progress to the United Nations (UN). In November 2009, the government published the *United Nations Convention on the Rights of the Child: Priorities for Action* (DCSF, 2009d), which is its latest plan.

The UK Government coordinates UNCRC, working with the devolved administrations in Wales, Scotland and Northern Ireland. When the government published its *Priorities for Action*, the Children's Commissioners for

England, Northern Ireland, Scotland and Wales issued a joint statement welcoming the government's achievements to date, while stressing that much remains to be done.

One of the government's *Priorities for Action* is to continue to make children and young people more aware of their rights. The primary-aged pupils at Hounslow Town Primary School in London, are very aware of UNICEF's *Little Book of Children's Rights and Responsibilities* (2007) and have used it to design their own charters.

Case study: Hounslow Town Primary School

Hounslow Town caters for 450 pupils aged 3–11. It is about to expand to become a three-form entry primary school. It has a very high proportion of children for whom English is an additional language (EAL). It is one of three primary schools in the borough that has a Centre for statemented pupils. The one at this school caters mainly for pupils who have moderate learning difficulties (MLD).

Like the school as a whole, the Centre has had several increases in size and it has recently been moved from being on the fringes of the school to occupying a more central position. As the Centre has grown, staff have been careful to take a personalised approach to each child's needs, so that pupils spend varying amounts of time in peer group classes, combined with receiving more intensive support within the Centre. The move to the middle of the building has made it easier for pupils to feel fully included in all aspects of the life of the school.

The *UNICEF booklet* (2007) is displayed in every classroom. This has helped pupils to become familiar with it, so that they have been able to make suggestions about a charter for their own classes. These charters specify the class rules in terms of rights and responsibilities. Each classroom has information displayed in a similar manner. As well as the charter, there is a Council Display Board with the names of class representatives and information about the current topics being discussed.

The school has gained *The Rights Respecting School Award* (RRSA), which was started by UNICEF UK in 2004 and is now running in more than 1000 primary and secondary schools in England, Wales, Scotland and Northern Ireland. It helps schools to use UNCRC as a values framework, contributing to many aspects of a school's work, including community cohesion, sustainable development and the global dimension.

Hounslow Town Primary is an example of a school that has not only done some imaginative work on pupil voice, but which has also embraced change in a number of ways. It has daycare provision run by a private provider, a nursery and a children's centre all on-site. It is the hub school for a cluster of 17 schools in an extended schools consortium. The extended schools coordinator has her office in the school and is line managed by the head teacher, Chris Hill, who says the school has always accepted the need for change and tried to respond positively to it.

Following on from their work on class charters, the pupils at Hounslow Town used the same idea to work together on creating a playground charter. This is shown as a photocopiable resource in Chapter 6 (Figure 6.1).

Tellus surveys

As further evidence of the feeling that more needed to be done about listening to children and young people, the Children Act (DFES, 2004a) created the position of children's commissioner, to have someone whose sole job it is to listen to children and to represent their views and interests on the wider stage. In addition to the commissioner's work, the Tellus surveys are another method of collecting views.

 Key points: The Tellus Survey

This is an annual, national survey that is used to gather views from a sample of children and young people about their life, their school and their local area. The questionnaires are answered online.

Children with SEND can have individual support in answering the questions and in the 2009 version, three formats for viewing the questionnaire were added:

- a **symbol survey** where the questions are displayed using Widget symbols to help pupils who are used to symbols rather than words
- a **British Sign Language (BSL) survey** with video clips of the questions being presented in BSL for pupils who are hearing impaired and use BSL as a mode of communication
- a **talking survey** where there is an audio recording of the questions for pupils with a visual impairment, a reading difficulty or for those with English as an additional language.

The voice of pupils with SEND

Working in partnerships with pupils not only aids their academic progress, but knowing that they are able to influence what happens, adds to their sense of well-being. This is important for all pupils, but particularly so in the case of pupils with SEND, some of whom will find it hard to express their thoughts and ideas.

Grangewood School in Pinner is a school for pupils who have very complex needs, including severe learning difficulties (SLD), profound and multiple learning difficulties (PMLD) and autism. Two thirds of the children are from minority ethnic backgrounds and nearly half speak English as an additional language. The school has gone to great lengths to make sure children and young people who have significant needs are able to express their views and influence how the school is run. The school's speech and language therapist worked with the children to find ways of helping each individual to express his or her own thoughts about the school and what it should be like. This resulted in the school's Ten Golden Rules, where the pupils' ideas have been put into words that reflect their perspective. The head teacher, John Ayres, explains that the Ten Golden Rules form the foundation for the ethos of the school. The rules are prominently displayed throughout the building, ensuring that the work of the staff is always child-centred. They are used as the basis for training staff who are joining the school and for young people who are taking up apprenticeships there.

Grangewood School's Ten Golden Rules

1. Treat me with respect and dignity
2. Talk to me, not about me
3. Listen to what I have to say
4. Allow me to make choices and decisions for myself
5. Give me time to respond and interact in my own way
6. Stay calm with me even if I do not stay calm myself
7. Let me know what's going to happen
8. Help me to stay safe
9. Try to understand me, I cannot explain my feelings
10. Telling me what I am good at builds my confidence

It takes time to elicit the views of children and young people whose understanding and use of language are very limited, and it is all too easy to think they cannot contribute, but, given the opportunity, and with the understanding of the adults who support them, ways can be found of giving pupils whose ability to express themselves is extremely limited, more say in their own lives, in terms of exercising a degree of choice and in voicing their opinions about their school and how it should operate.

School councils

Student councils have been common in secondary schools for some time, but are now becoming usual in primary and special schools as well. Some schools hold class council meetings as well as ones for representatives across the whole school.

Many school councils are given responsibility for spending a budget. One of the most common ways this is spent is on redesigning the school playground. At one school, it was a member of the council who pointed out that the new design did not include anywhere to sit down. He suggested that some children wanted to be able to sit quietly rather than rush around. As a result of his input, the school council was asked to make a presentation to the Parents and Friends Association (PFA). The PFA was so impressed by the thought that had gone into the presentation, that it was agreed to provide additional money for outdoor seating.

At another school, it was the facilities for staff who smoked which stirred the school council into action. Its members objected to the smokers' shelter being sited too near to the school, where it was in full view of the pupils. A campaign was launched through the student council to get it moved. This resulted in the shelter being re-sited some distance away, which not only pleased the pupils, but probably deterred the smokers, who now have to walk some distance in all weathers if they choose to smoke.

Pupils' wider involvement

School councils are one way in which schools are trying to take into account pupils' views on a whole range of matters and they bring a perspective that can shed fresh light on a situation. There are other ways, too, in which schools try to involve pupils more, both in their own learning and in thinking what will improve the school as a whole from the pupils' point of view.

Helen Clegg, the head teacher of Shiremoor Primary School, was determined to raise the aspirations of her pupils, many of whom come from a disadvantaged area of Newcastle. As well as a breakfast club, children who need it are given a second breakfast of milk and fruit mid-morning, to keep up their energy levels. Not only is the school council, which is called the Stay Safe and Happy Management Committee, taken very seriously, but class discussions dictate the way that the classrooms are organised. Feedback from pupils is an ongoing process and a suggestions box sits in the front entrance. A simple pro forma makes it easy for pupils of any age to jot down, or draw, both positive and negative comments about the school, as well as any ideas for improvement.

 Case study: Shiremoor Primary School, Newcastle

Shiremoor has around 450 pupils aged 4–11. The school has a number of ways of involving pupils in decision making and of giving them some responsibility for maintaining good standards of behaviour.

Stay Safe and Happy Management Committee (school council)

This is the school's equivalent of a school council, but it operates more as a committee. The name helps class representatives to realise the value of what they do in making decisions that will affect the safety and happiness of their peers. Although a member of staff chairs the meetings, the discussions are pupil-led and the class representatives have notebooks and are expected to take notes, so that they can report back in full to their classes. They cover a wide range of issues that pupils raise. One complaint, for instance, was from pupils complaining that parents were bringing dogs on to the playground and that this was becoming a health and safety issue. It was decided that members of the committee would write letters to the people concerned. This resolved the situation.

Encouraging good behaviour

The school has developed several strategies for making sure pupils feel they have responsibility for their own behaviour and for that of their peers. Classrooms are arranged with the tables round the edges, leaving a space in the middle for circle time, which is integrated into the daily timetable. Children discuss openly any issues that concern them. Each week, classes vote on who should receive an Excellent Behaviour Award. These are given out by the class representatives.

The school has a buddying system. Older pupils who want to be Buddies have to write a letter of application and then they are interviewed for the role. Sometimes pupils who have had problems with behaving appropriately themselves when younger, turn out to be understanding Buddies and, as well as helping younger pupils, develop a newly discovered sense of responsibility themselves.

Involving pupils in learning

As well as being written in their books, pupils are given badges with their targets written on them. This means that staff and other children can stop and talk to them about what they are learning, as well as being a constant reminder to the wearer of the badge. Every Autumn Term, when parents or carers come to the school to discuss their child's progress, the pupils attend for the last part of the interview and they are expected to be able to talk about what they can do and what they need to learn next.

Another school that encourages pupil involvement in a variety of ways is St Vincent's in Liverpool, which has been a school for the blind and partially sighted since 1841. In 2007, the school had the opportunity to become a specialist school with a specialism in sensory impairment. This has enabled it to develop fresh links with other schools. As the Principal of a non-maintained school, Steve Roberts has always been keen to remove any barriers between the state and non-maintained sectors and to be in a position to share the school's expertise in the field of visual impairment with other schools. For example, in 2009, St Vincent's collaborated with the primary schools in the West Derby Learning Community, to celebrate the International Year of Braille, which Steve Roberts said the schools found to be 'a most inclusive and awareness raising experience'.

 Case study: St Vincent's School – A Specialist School for Sensory Impairment and Other Needs, Liverpool

St Vincent's was established as a school for the blind and partially sighted in the 19th century. Today, it is a non-maintained school for 50 pupils aged 4–19. It caters for day, residential and extended day placements. In common

(Continued)

(Continued)

with many other special schools, St Vincent's takes pupils who have a range of other needs as well as their visual impairment.

The idea of pupil voice has a very high profile in the school. It is an item on every staff meeting agenda and some of the changes the school makes are in response to ideas put forward by pupils. For instance, the older pupils decided that they did not like the merit system, whereby they would be awarded points towards a reward. This system still operates for the younger pupils who respond well to it, but for older pupils, there is a letter of commendation that goes to their families, which they find much more motivating.

The school council is led by the pupils and everyone becomes involved in its work. It is promoted in assemblies and the agenda publicly announced. Council meetings are timetabled to take place during the school day. Pupils from the age of six upwards act as council representatives and those who take their turn as Chair learn the skills involved in chairing meetings. In addition, everyone learns to respect the views of others, regardless of their age. If staff want matters discussed, they will ask for items to be put on the agenda as well. Once a year, the pupils run the school instead of the staff. Teaching posts are advertised in advance, applications are made from those who want to lead classes and interview panels are set up. The pupils often express surprise at how much is involved in making appointments. This is quite apart from the amount they learn through managing the school for a day. The success can be measured by the fact that this has happened for many years and, each time, a different set of students has the opportunity to become teachers and to run the school.

Schools like St Vincent's are few and far between, as the number of children and young people whose visual impairment means that they need to be in a school designed around their needs, are few in number. By taking non-maintained schools into the specialist schools programme, expertise and resources can be more widely shared. Currently, independent schools are outside the programme, although some school leaders of independent special schools would like to be included. Certainly, it seems a waste not to be able to draw on specialist knowledge wherever it resides. (Further information on mainstream and special schools with a SEN specialism is given in the next chapter).

Valuing the voice of the child

Some people worry that the concept of pupil voice has gone too far and that pupils are being involved in matters outside their experience, such as having a role in the appointment of a new head teacher. However, the drive to see students as active participants, is generally accepted as being a factor in motivating them to learn, as well as giving them a greater sense of belonging to their school community. This is particularly important for pupils with SEND, who can more easily lose motivation or feel on the fringe of events. Children sometimes have a very clear insight into their own situation. A ten-year-old girl with epilepsy wrote in a school publication:

> The doctors found out I had epilepsy when I was seven. After a year and a bit I got very embarrassed but not now. No-one is perfect. Epilepsy is not who I am, it is just a bit of me.

 Questions for reflection

1. What do you see as the advantages of making pupils feel more engaged with how a school is run?
2. What do you see as the limits to pupil involvement? Should pupils, for instance, be involved in appointing staff?
3. Do you think progress has been made in recognising the voice of the child in the school or setting you know? Is there anything else you think would help the children to feel more involved in decision making?

Parental Involvement

There was a time when parents were actively discouraged from being involved in their child's education, as this was seen to be the sole responsibility of the school. It has taken time for both parents and schools to recognise the value of working together. Many schools welcome parents as volunteers, particularly in primary and special schools. Some of the more formal mechanisms that enable parents to contribute to the work of the school are through school governorships, being on a parent council or belonging to a Parent Teacher Association (PTA).

Parent bodies

Parent governors

The number of parent governors on a school's governing body has increased over the years, although it is not always easy to fill all the places. As the expectations of schools have increased, so has the workload of governing bodies. Nevertheless, it is a powerful way of understanding the school from the inside and contributing to its development. Parents who are able to focus on the development of the whole school rather than being concerned primarily with the needs of their own child, can be a strength on a governing body, as they have a vested interest in seeing the school develop and improve.

Parent councils

These are a newer development. Parent councils are run by and for parents and can be the means by which governing bodies communicate and consult with the parent body. Even with the increase in parent governors, there will only be a handful of places available, whereas parent councils can provide a role for as many parents as want to be involved. While the new breed of trust schools are required to have a parent council if the majority of the governing body is appointed and not elected, other schools can decide whether or not to have a parent council.

Parent Teacher Associations (PTAs)

PTAs have been around for many years and exist in some form in the majority of schools. They have helped to build better relationships between parents and staff, as they can work together in a more informal way than on a governing body. Most PTAs concentrate on putting on social events and fundraising for additional items that the school budget does not cover. Sometimes, staff are less involved and the association is made up of parents and friends of the school.

Systems for supporting parents

As the government has increased the amount of support to parents, there has been some confusion about the roles of the staff who work with parents. While parent partnership coordinators have been in existence since the 1990s, choice advisers and parent support advisers are newer roles.

Parent Partnership Services (PPS)

Following the publication of the SEN Code of Practice (DFEE, 1994), the government offered funding to Local Education Authorities (LEAs) to help them set up parent partnership services (PPS). Today, such services are statutory and they cater specifically for parents and carers of children and young people who have special educational needs (SEN). Parent partnership coordinators can explain how the LA and school assess children's needs and who parents can talk to about any concerns they may have. All PPS, wherever they are based, are at 'arm's length' from the LA. The services they provide are confidential and expected to be impartial.

Parent support advisers (PSAs)

PSAs are a more recent development, which started as a commitment in *The Children's Plan* (DCSF, 2007). Since then, the role has been expanded nationally. Unlike parent partnership coordinators, PSAs work with families who need support of various kinds, rather than specifically with parents and carers of children with SEND. The role is less clearly defined than that of the PPS, but PSAs work with families who need additional support with, for instance, making sure their children attend school regularly and on time. In this role, there is some overlap with the work of education welfare officers (EWOs), who also work closely with schools and families to resolve attendance issues.

Choice advisers

Choice advisers were mentioned in the government's White Paper, *Higher Standards, Better Schools for All* (DfES, 2005a), with a view to having a network of choice advisers from 2008. The role is designed to support parents who need help in finding their way round the education system, particularly in relation to choosing schools. As part of this work, the advisers help parents and carers access information about schools, including Ofsted reports, school prospectuses and the achievement and attainment tables (popularly known as 'league tables').

While any additional support for families who need it must be welcomed, as more posts are created, it is important to ensure that roles and responsibilities are clearly defined. If it is not possible to define with clarity the responsibilities of any new post, it may be because there is either too much overlap with a post that already exists or because the role has not been properly thought through.

Parents of pupils with SEND

One of the most contentious areas is often between LAs or schools and parents who have children with SEND. As these are the pupils who may not be able to fit in with what is provided for the majority, but need additional resources, and as extra resources, whether in the form of staffing or equipment, cost money, it is not surprising that the relationship can be a difficult one. Some parents describe it as a fight to get what they feel their child needs and, for a few, this will mean taking their fight all the way to a tribunal.

In 2007, the House of Commons Education and Skills Committee (since renamed) published a report entitled *Special Educational Needs: Assessment and Funding*. The report queried whether it was sensible to have LAs responsible for assessing children's needs, as well as being responsible for the costs of any placement or support that is needed. In response to this report, the DCSF set up the *Lamb Inquiry* (2009h) to examine how parental confidence in the assessment and statementing process could be improved. Brian Lamb was not asked whether there was a better way of meeting children's needs, but to consider how to improve the current system, which has been in place since the 1981 Education Act.

The Lamb Inquiry

As part of his work, Lamb established eight innovative projects in different areas of the country to look at various ways of engaging parents in the decision-making process. The projects looked at activities such as parent partnership services, LA decision making, delegated budgets and provision management. Lamb published a number of interim reports before his final one, which was published in December 2009 (DCSF, 2009h).

Key points: The Lamb Inquiry (2008–09)

Innovative projects

- These ran from September 2008 to July 2009
- *Local Authorities' Learning from the Eight Projects* (a study by Lindsay and Peacey, 2009)

Interim reports

- *Review of SEN and Disability Information (April '09)* (DCSF, 2009i)
- *Inspection, Accountability and School Improvement (August '09)* (DCSF, 2009j)
- *Quality and Clarity of Statements (August '09)* (DCSF, 2009k)

Final report

- *The Lamb Inquiry: Special Educational Needs and Parental Confidence 2008/09* (DCSF, 2009h)

In his final report, Lamb expressed one of his chief concerns as being that 'The system should not be designed around the presumption of failure but support parents in helping children succeed' (2009: 5). Lamb makes an interesting point here. Although the value of early identification of needs followed by any necessary intervention is widely recognised to be crucial, as the criteria for being assessed or for being statemented get tougher, it is sometimes not until a child 'fails' that his or her needs are taken seriously and addressed. Lamb also highlights the differences in the way the system operates in different LAs. In his letter thanking Brian Lamb for his work (16 December 2009: 4), the secretary of state agreed with his view that the system works best when schools, LAs and parents 'operate in true partnerships'.

Even when schools, LAs and parents are trying to work together, the fact that the definition of special educational needs and disabilities is not clear-cut and that it represents a continuum, means that there is plenty of scope for arguing about whether or not a child *has* SEND. If there is agreement about that, then there may still be disagreement about the severity of his or her needs. For instance, in one school, a child might be seen as being at School Action (the first stage of the SEN Code of Practice); at another school, the same child might be considered to be in need of specialist advice or support and placed on the next level of School Action Plus; while a third school might consider he or she should have a formal assessment with a view to having a statement. The situation has been made more difficult by the number of disorders that are recognised, as well as the possibility of a child having co-existing conditions.

Questions for reflection

1. Do you think it is possible to make a clear distinction between children who are at school action, those who are on school action plus and those who are, or need to be, statemented? How would you define the difference between these three stages?
2. Do you think it has become harder to get a statement for a child and, if so, do you think this is a problem or a step forward?
3. If you were able to devise your own system, would you want to keep statements, or would you want a different system? If the latter, in what ways would your system be different?

Children and families

Although this chapter concentrated first on pupils and then on parents and carers, the division is obviously a rather artificial one. The *Children, Schools and Families Act* (DCSF, 2010) originally contained both a Pupil Guarantee and Parent Guarantee that were announced in the preceding White Paper, *Your Child, Your Schools, Our Future* (DCSF, 2009c). These set out both rights and responsibilities in a similar way to UNCRC. Although this part of the Act was lost in the run up to the general election, the title of the Act together with the ECM agenda, concentrated on viewing children and their families as a unit and both of them as being partners in the process of education. It has been a slow road to reach this point and there remains much work to be done, but subsequent chapters will help to clarify that establishing effective relationships with children, young people and their families lies at the heart of today's educational agenda. A marked step forward in bringing schools and families closer together has been the creation of children's centres, many of which are attached to schools, and the move to create extended schools. Chapter 5 has case studies that demonstrate how these changes have helped to include families and their children in the process of learning, while, at the same time, providing easier access to the other services that may be needed, particularly by those who have SEND.

☐ Summary

This chapter has looked at the move towards personalising learning and encouraging pupils to become actively involved in their education. Giving children a greater degree of choice in how and what they learn, is particularly important in motivating pupils with SEND.

Case studies were provided of schools that have found ways of giving prominence to the voice of pupils, so that their ideas can influence what happens to them and to their school communities.

(Continued)

(Continued)

The importance of involving parents and carers in their children's education and seeing them as partners in the learning process is now recognised. This has been apparent in the extra support put in place for parents, the work of the Lamb Inquiry and the move to giving schools an extended role, which will be discussed more fully in Chapter 5.

Further reading

Department for Children, Schools and Families (2008) *Personalised Learning: A Practical Guide.* Available at www.publication.teachernet.gov.uk

Department for Children, Schools and Families (2009) *United Nations Convention on the Rights of the Child: Priorities for Action.* Nottingham: DCSF Publications.

Department for Children, Schools and Families (2009) *The Lamb Inquiry: Special Educational Needs and Parental Confidence 2008/09.* Available at www.dcsf.gov.uk/lambinquiry

Department for Education and Skills (2006) *2020 Vision: Report of the Teaching and Learning in 2020 Review Group.* Nottingham: DfES Publications.

2

The creation of schools with a SEN specialism

> This is the first chapter to consider the shift towards schools working collaboratively and it does so from the perspective of individual schools reaching out to other schools in order to share experience and expertise. It traces:
>
> - the origins of outreach work from specialist provision in the 1980s
> - the emergence of advanced skills teachers (ASTs) and excellent teachers (ETs) in the 1990s
> - the impact of the Specialist Schools Programme.
>
> Case studies are given of both mainstream and special schools that have become specialist schools with a SEN specialism.

Over the last 30 years, there has been a huge shift towards schools supporting each other rather than concentrating solely on their own students. This approach gathered momentum with the arrival of the Specialist Schools Programme and the advent of advanced skills teachers (ASTs). Before this, there were few recognised ways of schools reaching out to neighbouring schools, although there were many informal arrangements in existence. One exception was the Technical and Vocational Education Initiative (TVEI), which was rolled out nationally after a successful pilot. Aimed at improving the skills of 14–18-year-olds and making them better prepared for a world of work that was rapidly changing, it operated in some schools and colleges from 1987 to 1997. Many regretted it when it came to an end. Although not designed with the aim of bringing schools closer together, it led to schools collaborating in order to develop the programme. Apart from this, there were several instances of ad hoc arrangements, such as outreach work from special schools and other forms of specialist provision.

Outreach work from special schools

From the 1980s onwards, some special schools have been engaged in outreach work. The impetus for this work came from the growing number of pupils who were being integrated into mainstream schools in the wake of the 1981 Education Act. However, at this time, there was no organised drive to utilise the skills of special school staff or to match them to mainstream schools that were feeling the need of additional support, nor was there any recognised funding to sustain the work. Despite these limitations, outreach work began to be seen as a way that practising teachers across the sector divide could work together to meet the needs of pupils with special educational needs and disabilities (SEND). Such collaboration remained patchy, until the government's SEN strategy, *Removing Barriers to Achievement* (DfES, 2004b), appeared many years later.

The strategy, while expecting the trend for more pupils with SEND to be in mainstream schools to continue, recognised that special schools would be needed for the foreseeable future. The strategy gave special schools a continuing role, that would have a dual dimension: educating pupils with the most complex needs and supporting mainstream schools through developing outreach services. So, after 20 years or so of individual schools and local authorities (LAs) pioneering this type of work, it gained official approval.

As mainstream schools began to adapt to cater for a wider range of needs and an increasing number developed specialist units or bases, other kinds of specialist provision began to take on an outreach role as well. The recognition of the role did not necessarily solve the problem of funding, although some LAs recognised its value and funded it accordingly. Nor was there any guidance on how outreach work should complement the work of LA SEN advisory services. In the growing number of unitary authorities, this was less of a problem, as smaller LAs find it difficult to maintain a range of advisers. In larger authorities, there was more of a need to clarify where the boundaries lay between outreach teachers, SEN advisory teachers and also educational psychologists (EPs). It was not a question of insufficient work to go round, but of clarifying roles and responsibilities. These issues were partly addressed with the publication of the DCSF's *Quality Standards for Special Educational Needs (SEN) and Support and Outreach Services* (2008a), which, in addition to setting out 16 standards for these services, produced a model for planning, developing and commissioning them as well.

〰 Questions for reflection

1. Do you see a continuing role for special schools as part of a continuum of provision?
2. Can you envisage a time when mainstream staff have the skills to meet the whole range of needs?
3. Where outreach and advisory services exist in the same authority, how would you define their roles so that they are complementary?

The way the TVEI programme developed and the rise of outreach work are just two examples of how schools prefer to take a collaborative approach and to learn from each other, which persisted despite successive governments' emphasis on competition as the way to drive up standards. While a strong element of competition remains, there has been a growing recognition by government that schools working in partnerships, with each other and with other bodies, can accomplish more than schools working on their own, particularly in an age when so much is expected of them.

Advanced Skills Teachers (ASTs) and Excellent Teachers

In the 1990s, as well as the introduction of specialist schools (which will be considered shortly), the government introduced a new category of teacher: the Advanced Skills Teacher or AST. This was followed by the Excellent Teacher (ET) scheme. The schemes are open to secondary, primary and special schools, although the largest take-up has been in secondary schools. The aim is similar to that of the work of specialist schools, in spreading expertise and effective practice across schools. Both the AST and ET schemes identify teachers who have reached a high standard in the teaching of certain subject areas.

 Key points: ASTs and ETs

Advanced Skills Teachers (ASTs)

ASTs have to pass a national assessment and then be appointed to an AST position. The expectation is that they will spend 80% of their time in their own school and 20% working in neighbouring schools. By 2005, there were over 4000 ASTs and the number has continued to rise, with some schools employing a significant number of ASTs.

Excellent Teachers

The Excellent Teachers scheme has been less popular. The main difference is that these teachers spend all their time raising standards in their own schools rather than working in other schools as well. In some schools, there has been a reluctance to single out teachers in this way.

Both schemes strengthen teaching and learning, by encouraging some of the most talented practitioners to remain in the classroom, while demonstrating effective practice in their own schools, and, in the case of ASTs, to other schools as well.

The emergence of specialist schools in the 1990s began a run of changes that altered the face of secondary schools in particular, but which affected primary schools as well. In succeeding chapters, many of the different partnerships that exist between schools and between schools and other organisations, will be explored. The current chapter focuses on what individual schools are doing to link with their neighbours, for instance, through becoming specialist schools.

The Specialist Schools Programme

The forerunners of specialist schools were the City Technology Colleges (CTCs) created by Kenneth Baker, now Lord Baker, when Margaret Thatcher was Prime Minister. The CTC programme was established by the Education Reform Act 1988. Thatcher's idea was to have a network of inner city schools that were independent of local education authorities (LEAs), with wealthy industrialists being asked to provide £1 million towards building each new school. However, as there were not as many affluent philanthropists in the business world as Thatcher had hoped, only 14 CTCs were opened in urban areas across England in the period 1988 to 1993, plus one city college for technology and the arts (CCTA). They cater for pupils aged 11 to 18. The purpose of the CTCs was to provide a broadly based secondary education with a strong technological element, offering a wider choice of secondary schools to inner city pupils and providing them with a curriculum geared towards the world of work.

In 1993, the Conservatives tried to get more CTCs off the ground by instituting the Technology Colleges Programme. This allowed some secondary schools to specialise in technology, science and mathematics, provided they could raise £100,000 from business sponsorship. CTCs still exist, as does the CCTA. Their intakes are representative of the full range of ability among pupils in their catchment areas, from which they try to attract those who are most likely to benefit from the college's emphasis on science and technology. CTCs, like academies, (which are described in more detail in Chapter 4), are independent of the LA and funded directly by government, through a funding agreement with the secretary of state. Currently, Lord Baker has been instrumental in getting University Technical Colleges off the ground, again offering a more practical curriculum to 14–19 year olds.

The emergence of specialist schools

When Labour returned to power, it built on the CTC model to develop the Specialist Schools Programme, with the aim of enabling secondary schools to become centres of excellence in their chosen specialism, contributing towards raising educational standards, both in their own schools and in neighbouring ones as well. Specialist schools vary from CTCs in having a wider range of subject areas from which to select. The sponsorship money that has to be raised has been reduced, and additional funding comes from the government. Some specialist schools use the term *college* rather than *school*. As mentioned in the introductory chapter, although they are allowed to select up to 10% of their pupils on their aptitude for the subject in which the school or college is specialising, only a minority have chosen to do so.

By 1997, more than 200 specialist schools were in existence and by 2005, the target of 2000 specialist schools was met 18 months early. At the present time, there are over 3000 specialist schools, which is well over 90% of all secondary schools. Although the additional money is likely to be a draw, some head teachers maintain that it is the focus on innovation that is the main attraction, as well as being able to work in partnership with colleagues in other schools.

Coordinating the work of the growing number of specialist schools was the responsibility of the Specialist Schools Trust (SST). When the academies programme started, the SST became the Specialist Schools and Academies Trust (SSAT). When trust schools came on the scene, the SSAT took on responsibility for them as well, but did not alter its name again. Specialist status is not open to primary schools, although a few of them have been involved in a pilot. The Conservatives have said that they are interested in primary schools also receiving specialist status.

When specialist schools first started appearing, there were concerns that they would create a two-tier system, with specialist schools being seen as superior to secondary schools without a specialism, but, as the majority of secondary schools have achieved specialist status, this concern has diminished. The Labour government made it clear that it wanted all secondary schools to become specialist schools, academies or trust schools. This idea is likely to be supported regardless of which political party is in power. It is not that the comprehensive ideal has been disregarded, rather that the notion of all schools being similar has been replaced with a desire for a diversity of schools that will still remain comprehensive in their intake and outlook, but which will have their own distinctive ethos.

Schools can become specialist schools or colleges in ten different curriculum areas, either singly or in combination. In addition, schools may choose to have a SEN specialism.

Schools with a SEN specialism

The SEN specialism strand was introduced in 2005, when 12 special schools with secondary-aged pupils (all-age special schools or secondary special schools) were invited to become trailblazers for extending the specialisms that schools could have, to include a specialism in any of the four areas of need specified in the revised SEN Code of Practice (DfES, 2001b), namely:

- Communication and Interaction
- Cognition and Learning
- Behaviour, Emotional and Social Development
- Sensory and/or Physical Needs.

In addition to special schools being able to have a SEN specialism, mainstream secondary schools are also able to gain specialist status in the same four areas of need, provided that they already have specialist school status, through having one or more curriculum specialisms.

Key points: Specialist status

Curriculum specialisms

Any maintained secondary school and any maintained or non-maintained special school with secondary-aged pupils in England can apply for specialist status in one of ten curriculum areas. Some schools have added a second or even third specialism.

SEN specialisms

More recently, SEN specialisms have been introduced in one of the four areas of need set out in the revised SEN Code of Practice (DfES, 2001b). These are open to maintained and non-maintained special schools with secondary aged pupils and to mainstream secondary schools that already have one or more curriculum specialisms.

The invitation to apply for specialist status is not open to independent schools, whether or not they are special schools.

Specialist schools that achieve excellent results are recognised as high-performing specialist schools (HPSS). This means that further options are open to them, in addition to curriculum and SEN specialisms.

Case studies of schools with a SEN specialism

Whereas special schools have been eager to take on a SEN specialism, for mainstream schools, it has been a rather different story. In the present climate of how schools are judged, it is understandable that many mainstream schools will have concerns about becoming recognised as having a SEN specialism. To date, only 14 have taken on a SEN specialism. The numbers of schools for the four different areas of need divide up as follows:

Cognition and Learning   60
Communication and Interaction   54
Physical and Sensory Impairment   30
Behaviour, Emotional and Social Difficulties   21

A mainstream school with a SEN specialism in communication and interaction

One of the few mainstream secondary schools that has embraced the idea of having a SEN specialism is St Marylebone in Westminster, which is a voluntary controlled (VC) school for girls. The school already had two other specialisms before acquiring its SEN specialism in the area of communication and interaction. The school has always had a welcoming attitude to pupils who have additional needs, including those who have learning difficulties, those with social difficulties and those learning English as an additional language. There are separate support systems in place for them. No pupil has been permanently excluded for the last 14 years, due to having the mechanisms and staffing to operate internal exclusions when necessary.

The head teacher, Elizabeth Phillips, says that absorbing numerous developments has been made possible by staff not being territorial or defensive about their positions. Instead, they respond positively to innovation and are happy for roles and responsibilities to shift to meet new demands. She has no qualms about the school being recognised as a SEN college, but embraces the idea as an opportunity to help her students to have the right attitude when they move on and to be in a position to set an example.

 Case study: The St Marylebone School – A Specialist Arts, Maths, Computing and SEN College

St Marylebone is a voluntary-aided secondary school for 900 girls aged 11 to 18. Boys are accepted into the sixth form. The school was founded over 200 years ago and serves an area of social disadvantage. A very high number of pupils are entitled to free school meals and about half of the students speak English as an additional language.

In 1998, St Marylebone became a Specialist Arts College. In 2006, it added Maths and Computing to its other specialism. Having become a High Performing Specialist School (HPSS), in September 2008 the school was awarded a SEN specialism in the area of communication and interaction.

Having had the experience of establishing two other specialisms, the school leadership team had a very clear idea of how to embed its newest specialism. This is being achieved by making the process manageable for all concerned by taking it a step at a time. The first step has been to establish, with the help of the speech and language therapist, a database of pupils in Year 7 who have difficulties in the area of communication and interaction; to describe the nature of those difficulties; and to set out targets to address those needs. This will also be done with subsequent Year 7 cohorts as they join the school, so that, in time, the whole school will be covered. Heads of department make reference to these targets in their schemes of work, but concentrate on one subject at a time. Progress is monitored and moderated by staff from the SEN Team.

In addition to the work being done with its own students, some of the school's Advanced Skills Teachers (ASTs) have been working closely for some time with the two special schools in the borough, with the aim of establishing joint sixth form provision from September 2010. The pupils will be on the roll of one of the special schools, but receive most of their education at St Marylebone. With all the staff having received training in communication and interaction, it will make it easier for the curriculum to be presented in ways that the students from the special schools can access. Through this partnership, students from the special schools will have access to wider opportunities, while still receiving the support they need to maximise their abilities. The students at St Marylebone will gain a better understanding of those who have difficulty learning and communicating

(Continued)

(Continued)

and they will be in a position to offer the students from the special schools a wider circle of friends.

The school produces two types of newsletters. One is a general newsletter for parents and the other is Marylebone School Specialisms Newsletter, where the work of the school in all three specialist areas is celebrated. This is just one example of how the school has managed to integrate its three very different specialisms.

Having an inclusive ethos, keeping exclusions to a minimum and meeting a wide range of needs, has resulted in having a multi-disciplinary team of staff which includes: a school nurse who has additional hours, a speech and language therapist, two part-time psychotherapists, two members of the teaching staff who are also trained counsellors, staff who act as learning mentors for students who need extra support and guidance, trained peer mentors and two attached social workers. The head teacher sees the social workers as being necessary to enable teachers to concentrate on teaching and learning. In Chapter 6, Figure 6.6, there is a diagram showing how the communication and interaction strand of the school's work is woven horizontally across the whole of the school's management structure. This ensures that it is not seen as a separate strand, but is integrated into the staffing structure of the school, which Elizabeth Phillips describes as 'being like an amoeba that changes shape, rather than being concerned with status'.

 Questions for reflection

1. Do you think it is a good idea for both mainstream schools and special schools to be able to have a SEN specialism?
2. If so, what actions do you think should be taken to encourage more mainstream schools to seek this status?
3. Although the SEN specialism is available in the four areas of need listed in the SEN Code of Practice (DfES, 2001b), sometimes the five most prevalent areas (as in the Lamb Inquiry) are referred to as:

    •   Learning difficulties (LD)
    •   BESD
    •   Dyslexia
    •   Autism spectrum
    •   Speech, language and communication needs (SLCN).

Which list do you think it would be better to use in the context of SEN specialisms?

A special school with a SEN specialism in communication and interaction
Whereas mainstream schools with a SEN specialism are comparatively rare, special schools have seized the opportunity to become specialist schools in this area. Clearly, they are in a different position, as special schools, by the nature of their pupils, should be well placed to become recognised as specialists in the field of SEN.

Following the case study of St Marylebone, a mainstream school with a specialism in communication and interaction, the first special school example is of a school that shares the same specialist area. Corbets Tey School, in the London Borough of Havering, was quick to seize the opportunity of gaining a SEN specialism. It has a complex population of pupils and for many years the school has had a particular interest in the communication and interaction difficulties of its pupils. Some of the staff have been trained in the Verbal Behaviour approach, which is relevant to pupils who have significant communication difficulties, including those who are on the autism spectrum.

 Key points: Applied Behaviour Analysis (ABA) and Verbal Behaviour (VB)

Applied Behaviour Analysis (ABA)

In the 1960s, the psychologist B.F. Skinner was the originator of ABA, which stemmed from his idea of *operant conditioning* (1953), whereby desired behaviours are reinforced through rewards and undesirable ones are eliminated through negative reinforcers. This approach has been modified since then, with less emphasis on negative reinforcement.

Verbal Behaviour (VB)

In VB, language is broken down in a similar way and the child rewarded for a positive response, but the negative aspects of ABA are not part of the process. VB is based on the recognition that children who have specific or severe language impairments do not follow the usual developmental sequence for acquiring language, but have a very scattered pattern of skills development.

The approach looks first at what the child wants and then teaches the child how to request it. In this way, children learn that if they use verbal behaviour (that is to say, some form of communication), they will receive the item they want. To begin with, this may amount to no more than reaching for an item to indicate interest. In children who are pre- or non-verbal, signing is recognised as a means of communication. The activities are used in natural settings and they are child-led rather than adult-directed.

Some of the staff at Corbets Tey had been using this approach successfully for some time with their own pupils. Since gaining the SEN specialism, they have been using it in mainstream schools as well, for children who have significant difficulties in communicating or in interacting with other people.

Case study: Corbets Tey School – A Specialist College for Communication and Interaction

Corbets Tey is a special school for over 100 pupils aged 4 to 16 with a range of needs, including moderate or severe learning difficulties and additional language difficulties. More than half have been diagnosed as being on the autism spectrum. The school gained its SEN specialism in communication and interaction in 2007.

With the capital build allocation from its new status, the school has been able to build a Training Centre, with space for a speech and language therapy base, as well as a room for the Primary Care Trust (PCT) to hold clinics. The Training Centre houses a Language Resource Centre with an extensive range of:

- puppets and toys
- tactile and sensory books
- children's picture books and stories
- board games and card games
- CDs, speech and language resource books
- reference books.

All these resources can be borrowed by local schools. The main room is used for both training and meetings. Every week, there is a drop-in session for local schools, when they have access, at the same time, to the school's educational psychologist (EP), who specialises in speech and language, a speech and language therapist and an LA advisory teacher for speech and language. The room is also used by the Educational Psychology Service (EPS), the Social Services Disability Team and by neighbouring schools, so that the whole building has become a multi-professional resource for the area.

The school runs Aqua Language sessions, both for its own pupils and for other groups who can benefit. They are held in the school's large hydrotherapy pool, which has coloured lighting and streams of water from the ceiling to the surface of the pool. In this environment, some young children, who are reluctant to express themselves, become more receptive to the idea of communicating, as they want to share their experience and excitement.

From 2007 to 2009, the school worked in partnership with English Touring Opera. The culmination of this project was a performance of Speakout, a full-length extravaganza devised by the children in collaboration with a group of performers from the theatre company. All pupils were involved and they were on the stage of a local theatre throughout the full-length show, indicating how even those with normally very limited attention spans or understanding, were fully engaged by working alongside professional artists. There are plans for pupils from schools across the town to come together and perform songs from the show.

Although the school had been engaged previously in outreach work, this has expanded to incorporate the communication and interaction dimension, including introducing schools to Verbal Behaviour. The head teacher, Colin Arthey, is very keen to ensure that the school's emphasis on partnership working and on giving pupils the widest possible experiences, is maintained in the future. For this reason, he is working with a local high school, Hall Mead, and together they are exploring Trust status. A number of organisations have expressed interest in becoming partners, including a university, a football club, a hospice and four local primary schools. (Further information on schools that have already become trust schools is given in Chapter 4.)

A special school with a specialism in cognition and learning

After looking at two schools, one mainstream and one special, that have both acquired a SEN specialism in communication and interaction, the next school has a specialism in cognition and learning. Barrs Court was one of the first special schools to be awarded a SEN specialism. The school went for a specialism in cognition and learning, because of its experience in meeting the needs of a whole range of students, from those with moderate learning difficulties (MLD) right through to those with profound and multiple learning difficulties (PMLD). With some of its more complex pupils, the school uses a technique called *intensive interaction.*

 Key points: Intensive interaction

Intensive interaction was developed in the 1980s as a way of teaching the pre-speech fundamentals of communication to people who are still at an early stage of communication development. A communication or interaction partner (who might be, for instance, a carer, a teacher, a therapist or a family member) assists the person with learning difficulties to engage with them by following the learner's lead and responding to what they do.

By observing the learner's reactions and copying his or her activities, a relationship can be established and periods of intensive interaction lengthened. The sessions are designed to be frequent and quite intensive, but also to be playful and enjoyable. Over time, the fundamentals of communication may be established.

On gaining specialist status, the school decided to start by focusing on a curriculum that would be relevant to the most complex end of the SEN continuum.

 Case study: Barrs Court Specialist (SEN) School

Barrs Court came into existence following the Education (Handicapped) Children Act of 1970, which brought all children, including those with the

(Continued)

(Continued)

most complex needs, into the education system for the first time. The school caters for up to 80 pupils aged 11 to 19 who have:

- a profound and multiple learning difficulty (PMLD)
- a severe learning difficulty (SLD)
- an autistic spectrum disorder (ASD)
- a multi-sensory impairment (MSI).

The school has had specialist status since 2006. Some of the grant was used to improve and enlarge the teaching facilities in the older parts of the building, which was essential as 80 pupils were working in a space created for half that number. The revenue grant was used to form a new career structure for teaching assistants. A new layer at the top was created for Instructors in Disability. There are three of these posts and each postholder focuses on one of the three areas of communication, physical and sensory needs, acting as a champion for that area. The Instructors run training programmes for teaching assistants, to ensure that they are knowledgeable about pupils' communication, physical and sensory needs. Several teaching assistants have taken foundation degrees or taken the Graduate Teacher Programme (GTP) as a route to gaining qualified teacher status (QTS). The Instructors are also responsible for linking with families and foster carers. They carry out some of the outreach work in local schools.

In addition, Barrs Court sells the materials it has created from its work on cognition and learning. Already, these materials have been purchased by a large number of schools, which allows Barrs Court to plough the money back into the development of further work on cognition and learning. The materials offered to schools include:

- an Early Thinking Skills Curriculum
- an Early Communication Skills Curriculum
- an Early Mobility Curriculum
- an Early Emotional Literacy Curriculum.

Considerable research and thought has gone into the creation of these materials, in order to make them appropriate for those who are teaching pupils who have PMLD, each one of whom will have his or her own particular combination of sensory impairments, motor disabilities and medical problems. A contents list for one of these resources is given as a photocopiable resource in Chapter 6, Figure 6.7. The final one, on Emotional Literacy, is still being developed.

The head teacher, Richard Aird, describes the curriculum at the school as including the national curriculum, but being much broader than that. He points out that special schools should have something extra to offer its pupils. 'We need to be demonstrably different', he says, 'or there is no point in our existence'. Alongside revamping the school's schemes of work, previous progress measures for pupils with MLD, SLD and PMLD have given way to level descriptors, so that every tiny step a pupil takes can be recorded and plotted against the P levels, or for more able pupils, the lower levels of the national curriculum. In this way, the progress of all pupils, including those who have the most complex needs, can be measured.

Barrs Court is also a Trust School, having been invited by the DCSF to become an early adopter of Trust status. After first becoming a foundation school, in September 2009, Barrs Court became a Trust School, with a large number of partners. These include the Royal National Institute for the Blind (RNIB), with which the school hopes to develop joint post-16 provision in a separate building, for students whose degree of learning difficulty means that the ordinary college courses are not accessible. Another partner is The Elms School, which is the oldest preparatory school in England, with day and boarding provision for girls and boys aged eight to thirteen years and a pre-prep department for three- to seven-year-olds. Barrs Court pupils benefit from being able to use some of The Elms' extensive facilities, while the head teacher of The Elms feels it is important for his pupils to gain a better understanding of pupils who have disabilities. This is an interesting partnership between a maintained special school and an independent school.

A special school with a specialism in behaviour, emotional and social difficulties (BESD)

The final case study in this chapter focuses on Shaftesbury High School in Harrow, which, as well as being a special school with a SEN specialism, is co-located with Hatch End High School and Arts College, a mainstream school for 1400 students. Currently, a swimming pool is being built on the site, which will be a shared facility between the Hatch End and Shaftesbury schools. (There is further information about co-located schools in the next chapter).

Both Shaftesbury and Hatch End share an interest in pupils with SEND. Hatch End is additionally resourced for deaf students, while its Inclusion Unit supports students at risk of exclusion, those whose medical needs result in long periods of absence and those who require emotional support. Originally designated as a school for pupils who have MLD, the specialism Shaftesbury High School chose was behaviour, emotional and social difficulties (BESD), with the emphasis being on pupils' emotional development. The head teacher of Shaftesbury, Paul Williams, felt that a focus on emotional difficulties would build on the school's work in relation to its changing population. As he points out, every child has emotional needs, which present themselves in a variety of ways, some of which call for additional support. The school has worked closely with the Child and Adolescent Mental Health Service, (CAMHS). In 2007, the DCSF and the Department of Health set up an independent review of CAMHS to look at how children's emotional well-being and mental health needs were being supported and how this support might be improved.

Key points: The CAMHS Review

The findings of the CAMHS Review, *Keeping Children and Young People in Mind: The Final Report of the National CAMHS Review* (DCSF and DoH, 2008a) saw improvements in the service over recent years, but that the quality was variable and accessibility inconsistent. The government made an immediate response to the 20 recommendations, including setting up a National Advisory Council to help with the implementation of the findings and a National Support Programme to improve support for practitioners within the service.

In January 2010, the government made a fuller response, *Keeping Children and Young People in Mind: The Government's Full Response to the Independent Review of CAMHS* (DCSF and DoH, 2010), which uses examples of effective practice to encourage greater consistency and outlines the support the government is offering to assist the delivery of effective services.

Case study: Shaftesbury High School and BESD specialism

Shaftesbury High School in the London Borough of Harrow is a special school for 120 students aged 11–19 who have MLD, BESD, autism and a range of other needs. Just over half the students are from ethnic minority backgrounds, the largest group being from Asian families. The head teacher, Paul Williams, says:

> In view of having a wider and more complex range of students, I wanted to create an inclusive system within which every pupil received appropriate levels of support, and, to do this, we needed to create an environment where this could happen.

Over the years, the school has had several refurbishments and additions. Gaining the SEN specialism in BESD in 2007, enabled the head teacher to complete the move towards reorganising the school to meet current and projected needs by providing a base for students on the autism spectrum from September 2008.

With Harrow moving away from a middle-school system, from September 2010, the school obtained additional premises to provide:

- BESD provision (The Long Elmes Centre) from September 2010
- separate sixth-form accommodation (The Whittlesea Centre).

The extra provision for pupils with autism and The Long Elmes Centre for pupils with BESD will mean that the school is able to provide different environments for pupils whose emotional difficulties stem from being on the autism spectrum and for those whose emotional difficulties and resulting behaviours have different origins. Also from the autumn of 2010, the school is creating a new post for a Family Liaison Officer, whose role will be to offer emotional support to families.

As there is a close relationship between emotional well-being and pastoral care, one senior teacher is the Pastoral Care Manager, who line manages two learning mentors and acts as the link with social care. The role also includes responsibility for safeguarding and well-being. The school runs a counselling service for students and their families. Art therapy is available to pupils who can benefit from it and yoga classes have been found to have a calming effect on many of the students.

This year, the school became part of a two-year local authority project with CAMHS, to set up support groups for families, with the aim of raising the self-esteem of parents and their children.

The school's Professional Development Centre has developed additional courses on emotional development and pastoral care. These are attended by staff from other local schools and personnel from the LA.

Senior members of staff from both schools meet regularly to discuss the progress of pupils with SEND and to share ideas on trying out new approaches. At any one time, up to 20% of the students at Shaftesbury have the opportunity to be included in mainstream classes at Hatch End. If a pupil needs to move full-time, the transition process is eased by the two schools being able to work closely together in preparing a student for the move.

The only other SEN specialism that has not been covered in this chapter is the strand for sensory and physical needs. St Vincent School in Liverpool, which was mentioned in Chapter 1 for its work on pupil voice, is a non-maintained specialist school for sensory needs. As a result, its full name is St Vincent's School – A Specialist School for Sensory Impairment and Other Needs.

As mentioned in the introductory chapter, although a particular aspect of a school's work has been picked out for the purpose of the case studies, schools have many strands to their work. In this chapter, for instance, it was mentioned that Shaftesbury High School is also a co-located school, while Barrs Court is both a specialist school and a trust school. As the book unfolds, it is becoming clear that, not only are there an increasing number of types of schools, but that schools are taking on many different forms.

Summary

This chapter has examined the move away from competition between schools, to schools working in partnership. This shift has been apparent in outreach work from various types of specialist provision, from having ASTs, whose role includes working in neighbouring schools as well as their own, and, most notably, through the move to encourage all secondary schools to become specialist schools.

(Continued)

(Continued)

After discussing the history of specialist schools and their ability to choose from a range of curriculum specialisms, the focus switched to schools that have acquired a SEN specialism. Case studies were presented of schools that have specialisms in the four areas of need in the SEN Code of Practice.

While special schools have welcomed the idea of being recognised in this way, the competitive element which still exists has made it harder for mainstream schools to embrace the idea of having a SEN specialism.

Further reading

Department for Children, Schools and Families (2008) *Quality Standards for Special Educational Needs (SEN) and Support and Outreach Services*. Nottingham: DCSF Publications.

Department for Children, Schools and Families and the Department of Health (2008) *Keeping Children and Young People in Mind: The Final Report of the National CAMHS Review*. Nottingham: DCSF Publications.

Department for Children, Schools and Families and the Department of Health (2010) *Keeping Children and Young People in Mind: The Government's Full Response to the Independent Review of CAMHS*. Nottingham: DCSF Publications.

Nind, M. and Hewett, D. (2001) *A Practical Guide to Intensive Interaction*. Kidderminster: BILD Publications.

3

Partnership working between groups of schools

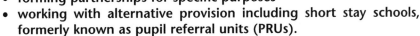

This chapter moves from looking at how individual schools are reaching out to form links with neighbouring schools, to a consideration of how groups of schools are working together through:

- being co-located
- forming federations
- forming partnerships for specific purposes
- working with alternative provision including short stay schools, formerly known as pupil referral units (PRUs).

The previous chapter looked at the partnerships individual schools have developed by running outreach services, appointing advanced skills teachers (ASTs) and becoming specialist schools. The present chapter moves the focus from the work of individual schools to looking at how groups of schools are working collaboratively. The chapter begins by looking at co-location and gives examples of schools and services that have been co-located. This is followed by information about federated schools and an example of three schools (primary, secondary and special) that are both co-located and federated. Before moving on to the last part of the chapter, there is a mention of some of the partnerships clusters of schools are forming for certain purposes, particularly the behaviour and attendance partnerships, which have recently become statutory for secondary schools. This leads into the final section on short stay schools (the name given to pupil referral units, or PRUs, from September 2010). The two case studies show contrasting ways of personalising learning for students who need an alternative approach to their education.

Co-located schools

'Co-location' is the term used when two or more schools share a site and work closely together. They may occupy separate buildings or be physically attached to each other. An increasingly common type of co-location is the bringing together of special and mainstream schools. Sometimes this is done as part of the Building Schools for the Future (BSF) programme, which has provided local authorities (LAs) with the opportunity to re-think the geographical location of their schools and the benefits of co-location. The Primary Capital Programme (PCP) is not as advanced as BSF and it is difficult to judge how far there will be scope to support the co-location of schools. Whereas BSF was established with the intention of replacing or refurbishing every secondary school in England, only half the primary schools were expected to be covered by the PCP.

 Key points: Renewing secondary and primary schools

Building Schools for the Future (BSF)

The BSF programme was started by the government in 2004. The original aim was to renew all 3500 secondary schools in England by 2020. This was to be achieved by rebuilding 50% of schools, remodelling 35% and refurbishing the rest. Partly due to the complexity of getting this extensive programme off the ground and partly due to a changing financial situation, the original scheme has been modified.

Primary Capital Programme (PCP)

The Primary Capital Programme (PSP) came on stream after BSF, with the aim of renewing half of all primary schools by 2022/23 and giving them space to include a wider range of services for children and families, so that they can fulfil their role as being at the heart of their communities.

It is apparent from the above description of the PCP that it is seen as a vehicle for co-locating other services within schools, in order to assist them in developing their extended role. (This role is explored further in Chapter 5). As both renewal programmes extend over many years, it is not clear how far the original aims will be fulfilled. Changes of government and tighter budgets mean that it is impossible to predict at this time the extent to which the programmes will be delivered.

The following examples of co-location come from Guernsey. One is of a mainstream secondary school being co-located with a special school for secondary-aged pupils. The other is a special school for primary-aged pupils which has been rebuilt with a centre for other services incorporated into the new building. As Guernsey does not benefit from the BSF programme, this was achieved as part of the States of Guernsey Education Department's ten-year capital building project. This was produced with the aim of creating twenty-first century learning environments for all pupils on the island.

Co-located schools in Guernsey

The following case study shows how Guernsey has encouraged partnership working, both between schools and between schools and services, by co-locating its two special schools.

 Case Study: Guernsey – Baubigny Schools and Le Rondin School and Centre

The Baubigny Schools in St Sampson's is the name given jointly to St Sampson's High School and Le Murier School, which opened in a single building in September 2008. The former is a mainstream secondary school for over 700 students aged 11–16, while Le Murier is a special school for up to 130 secondary-aged students who have a range of learning difficulties. A central block of facilities, including a cafeteria, sports hall, six-lane swimming pool, gym, climbing wall and a covered atrium are used by the students from both schools, as are the outdoor grass and synthetic sports pitches. The outdoor facilities are used by the local community out of school hours. Although each school has its own leadership team and retains its separate identity, the design makes it easy for the pupils and staff of both schools to interact and to share their experience and expertise.

Having ready access to the facilities and resources of a newly designed secondary school means that the pupils from Le Murier are able to enjoy a wider range of opportunities and activities than when they were at a separate school. The benefits for the mainstream students include getting to know the Le Murier students as individuals and gaining a better understanding of their needs, while students from Le Murier are able to attend mainstream classes to the degree that is appropriate for each individual.

Le Rondin is a special school for up to 150 primary-aged pupils. The school has been carefully designed to create an environment for children who have a whole range of special educational needs and disabilities (SEND). The school opened in its new building in 2005. Each of its three teaching wings has distinctive stained glass windows and a different colour scheme, to help pupils find their way around. The classrooms have been designed as flexible learning spaces, so that rooms can be divided or opened up as required. Each wing has access to the outside, with areas for play and outdoor learning, which the pupils have helped to create.

From the start, it was planned that the building would house both a school and a Centre that would bring together professionals from across the services. The accommodation in the Centre includes space for educational psychologists and the education support services, as well as the health service's child development centre (CDC) and rooms for therapists to work. This gives parents and carers from the community access to the professionals they may need to contact all under one roof.

It is interesting to note that, despite differences in the way the education service operates in Guernsey, similar developments to those that are happening in England are seen as important. The co-location of the Baubigny Schools has enabled the head teachers and staff of both schools to work together in a way that was not possible before and has opened up wider opportunities for all the students, as well as for the local community. While Le Rondin does not share a site with another school, it was built close to Forest Primary School which has enabled the schools to build close links between staff and pupils. In addition, the co-locating of services within Le Rondin gives ready access to a range of professionals, both for the pupils at Le Rondin (who have a higher level of need for interagency support) and for the wider community as well. This not only makes for easier access to recipients of the services, but increases the opportunities for professionals from different backgrounds to work as a multi-professional team.

Federations

There are many different styles of federations, in terms of the number and combination of schools that may be involved. There are two main types of federations. These used to be known as *hard* and *soft federations*, but hard federations are now referred to as *federations*, while the arrangements for soft federations are known as *collaborative governance*. Under the Education Act 2002, it became possible for more than one school to share a governing body, or alternatively, for schools to establish a form of collaborative governance, whereby one or more joint committees are given delegated powers.

 Key points: Co-location and federations

Co-located schools are ones that share a site. They may be physically attached, so that some areas are shared while separate identities are retained, or they may consist of two or more separate buildings on the same site.

Federated schools may share a site or they may be some distance from each other. There are two main types of federations:

- *Collaborative governance (soft federation)* refers to schools that keep their own governing bodies and establish a joint committee with some delegated powers.
- *Federation* (hard federation) describes schools that share a joint governing body. Although they still retain separate budgets, having a single body making decisions means that the process is much quicker.

Schools may be both co-located and federated.

The aspiration set out in the White Paper, *Your Child, Your Schools, Our Future: Building a 21st Century School System* (DCSF, 2009c) is for federations and other partnership solutions to become central to the school system. Already, schools are being judged on the quality of their partnership working, rather than just as individual establishments and Ofsted is looking at bringing into line the inspection of separate schools that are part of a federation. The government is encouraging LAs to co-locate their schools or to form federations when the opportunity arises, on the grounds that these are effective mechanisms for enabling schools to benefit from each other's expertise and for the pupils involved to have an enriched educational experience. On the other side of the argument, there are concerns that it can be seen as a money-saving exercise, where, for instance, a single head teacher looks after more than one school.

Darlington Education Village

The next case study is of a federation that is also a co-location of three schools. Darlington Education Village was one of the first federations to involve a primary school, a secondary school and a special school all under one roof and under one Executive Principal. It occupies the site of Haughton Community School, which was knocked down and rebuilt on the same site, together with two other schools. The Village was built, not through the BSF programme, but through the Private Finance Initiative (PFI).

 Key points: Private Finance Initiative (PFI)

The Private Finance Initiative (PFI) started in 1992. PFI is a form of public–private partnership (PPP) that increases the involvement of the private sector in the provision of public services. This enables LAs and others to gain access to new or improved capital assets, such as being able to build new schools and hospitals, without owning them. The private sector makes a capital investment in the asset and recovers their costs over 25 years or so, while the public sector pays for their use and associated services such as maintenance and cleaning.

The Village opened in April 2006 after many years of planning. It has now been established long enough to have experienced what it is like to go through such a massive change and to be able to realise the benefits for all concerned. Although under one roof, the schools have retained their names and separate identities. At the same time, The Village operates as a single community. The corridors are colour-coded so that children can find their way around and the signs on the classroom doors indicate whether or not the room has been adapted for pupils with the most complex needs. There are 1400 pupils who attend The Village. Both the secondary school and the special school are also specialist schools.

Case study: Darlington Education Village – Springfield Primary School, Haughton Community School and Beaumont Hill

Springfield is a primary school for 270 pupils aged 3–11. Haughton Community School has 900 students aged 11–16 and is an Arts College. Beaumont Hill is an all-age special school for 225 pupils aged 2–19, which has specialist status, both as a Technology College and in Applied Learning (formerly known as Vocational). It is also a Training School. Together, they make up the Darlington Education Village which opened in April 2006. All three schools benefit from sharing specialisms.

The schools are located in a single building around a space known as the Village Green, which is used for various school and community events. Although the building is on two floors, it has been made fully accessible, not only with lifts, but with outside ramps that slope all the way up to the first floor. The schools have 'home areas' as well as shared spaces across The Village.

The classrooms have been designed with extra floor space to accommodate wheelchair users and most of the rooms designed for teaching specific subjects have been fitted out to enable them to be used by children with the most complex needs as well. Some of these pupils spend most of the time in their own classrooms, but are still able to benefit from the huge range of facilities that the three schools between them provide. In addition, there is provision for a group of 40 students who do not respond to the normal school environment, to receive an even more personalised curriculum. A high level of staffing and an education tailored to their individual needs enables these students to remain in school, rather than finding themselves excluded.

The nearby children's centre uses The Village to deliver some of its programmes, including a Primary Care Trust (PCT) Clinic, Montessori Childcare and a Parent and Toddler Club. The Citizens Advice Bureau (CAB) is also available on site, so that the whole campus has the feel of a village, with people of all ages making use of the facilities throughout an extended day.

Being a federation, the schools have a single governing body that is responsible for the combined budget. The four committees mirror the objectives of Every Child Matters. A head of business strategy works across the schools, freeing up the leadership team to concentrate on teaching and learning. A strong sense of belonging to The Village has been created by designing a logo, having a uniform that is worn by children depending on their age rather than which school they attend, and holding joint training days for all staff. A termly newsletter, known as *The Village Green*, helps everyone connected with The Village, including families living in the area, to be kept in touch with events and activities.

In talking about the development of The Village, Dame Dela Smith, the Executive Principal and Head Teacher, says that this was an opportunity to do things differently, to provide a context for change, and a chance to work together with the child at the centre. She says that there were some initial concerns from parents, and a worrying time when the change was taking place. The primary and special school children took the change in their stride, but the secondary school students found it harder, partly because they had been unsettled by a series of changes before becoming part of The Village. Initially, exam results dropped, but now they have risen substantially and the benefits of creating the village community have become apparent. Dame Dela says:

> No-one is patronised or stared out. People have a right to be different. I believe in children who have the most complex needs being at the heart of a community. Every child in the area has a right to be part of The Village.

Forest Schools

Soon after it started, The Village acquired a forest five miles away, which it developed into a Forest School. Today, it has trees, rare plants and great crested newts (which are a protected species). A member of staff, who has trained as a Forest School Leader, is there full-time, making sure that the area is ready and safe for pupils between visits and preparing for the activities that will take place.

 Key points: Forest Schools

Forest Schools started in the 1990s, following models developed in Scandinavia. They provide a way of promoting children's physical, social and emotional development, as well as helping them to learn a range of skills through interacting with the natural environment.

A growing number of schools have cultivated their own forest areas in the school grounds, or linked with places nearby to provide pupils with an opportunity to engage with the natural world.

Forest schools are run by leaders who are trained to support children's learning outdoors. The idea is that it is not just a one-off visit, but enough time is spent in the environment for pupils to gain from the experience and to develop an awareness of the outdoors.

In her book, *Forest Schools and Outdoor Learning in the Early Years* (2009), Sara Knight points out that it used not to be necessary to create formal links between education and the outdoors, but with children spending less time outside and with many living in flats or homes without gardens, there is a renewed interest in the importance of outdoor education. In a Forest School, pupils usually spend a minimum of half a day a week there for at least ten weeks. There are courses for those who want to become Forest School leaders, which Knight describes in her book.

Questions for reflection

1. What do you see as the advantages of co-locating schools? What are the problems that might arise?
2. How many schools and what age phases would form your blueprint for a co-location or a federation?
3. Could the kind of arrangement described in the case study of Darlington Education Village lead to the phasing out of special schools? If so, would this be a good way forward or not?
4. What do you think should be the place of learning outside the classroom? Is it equally important for all age groups?

Partnerships between schools

Today it is accepted that, regardless of the other partnerships they may have, groups of schools will work together for particular purposes. Robert Hill, in his book, *Achieving More Together: Adding Value Through Partnership* (2008), is clear that partnerships help schools to move forward and to continue to improve. The number of partnerships that secondary schools, in particular, are expected to have, can be quite difficult for schools to manage, as different groupings of schools are needed for different tasks. For instance, a secondary school may be in a safer schools partnership, an extended schools cluster, a consortium for delivering the 14–19 diplomas and another for behaviour and attendance partnerships.

Behaviour and attendance partnerships

In 2005, Sir Alan Steer was asked by the DCSF to carry out a review of behaviour in schools. He produced a report entitled *Learning Behaviour* (DfES, 2005b) that made a series of recommendations. Three years on, the government asked him to review the progress that had been made. His updated report, *Learning Behaviour: Lessons Learned* (DCSF, 2009a) resulted in legislation, which meant that, under the Apprenticeships, Skills, Children and Learning Act (2009), secondary schools, including academies, are required to work together in school behaviour partnerships. Although the majority of secondary schools have operated like this for some time, it is now a legal requirement.

 Key points: Behaviour and attendance partnerships

These partnerships are formed by secondary schools in an area, often in conjunction with short stay schools and special schools, working collaboratively and pooling their resources, to support pupils whose behaviour and/or attendance is unsatisfactory. This helps to identify problems at an

> early stage. This shared approach enables pupils to receive a wider range of support than would otherwise be available. It can include a 'managed move', where schools within the partnership agree to give a pupil a fresh start in one of their schools.

Clearly, there is a close connection between the work of behaviour and attendance partnerships and the role of alternative provision. Although managed moves and sharing 'hard to place' pupils are ways of groups of schools addressing problems and arriving at a solution between them, there will still be occasions when a different solution has to be found.

Alternative Provision

Alternative Provision refers to education outside mainstream or special schools.

It takes many forms, including:

- short stay schools (known until September 2010 as pupil referral units or PRUs)
- Further education (FE) colleges
- extended work experience or vocational training
- projects provided by the voluntary or private sector
- multi-agency initiatives, such as the Youth Service.

It can be a means of re-engaging pupils who are disaffected, as well as supporting those who have been excluded or who are at risk of exclusion. Education outside of school can be commissioned by LAs or schools. It may include students spending time in more than one of the above environments. Excluded pupils or those at risk of being excluded form the largest group of students in alternative provision. However, provision also has to be made for those who cannot attend school for other reasons.

Short stay schools (formerly PRUs)

PRUs replaced the off-site units that existed in the 1970s and 1980s, which were seen as offering very variable standards of education. PRUs are often thought of as places where badly behaved children are sent, but, although they are best known for their work with those who have either been excluded or who are at risk of exclusion, they cater for other students as well.

Although PRUs had a much better record than the off-site units they replaced, the government had concerns about their variability and that of alternative provision in general. So, in 2008, a White Paper was issued entitled *Back on Track: A Strategy for Modernising Alternative Provision for*

Young People (DCSF, 2008f), which picked up on proposals made in *The Children's Plan* (DCSF, 2007). The White Paper was followed by a further publication, *Taking Back on Track Forward* (DCSF, 2008g), which suggested that the new name for PRUs would be 'short stay schools'. This was confirmed in the Apprenticeships, Skills, Children and Learning Act (DCSF, 2009e). In the ministerial foreword to the first of these documents, the secretary of state said that around 135,000 pupils a year, mostly of secondary age, spend time in some form of alternative provision and about one third of these students are in the 450 PRUs that existed at the time. Although some PRUs cater for younger pupils, over 90% of the students are aged 11–15 and nearly 70% are boys. 75% of pupils in PRUs have SEN and 13% have statements.

> **⊶ Key points: Short stay schools/Pupil Referral Units (PRUs)**
>
> PRUs are a type of school run by LAs to provide education for children who cannot attend school. Placing pupils in PRUs is one of the ways in which LAs can ensure that they comply with their duty under the Education Act 1996, to provide suitable education for children of compulsory school age who are unable to be in school.
>
> The Apprenticeships, Skills, Children and Learning Act (DCSF, 2009e) changed the name of PRUs to *short stay schools*. This change applies to England. In Wales, they will continue to be called PRUs. The idea of this change is to make it clear, firstly, that students are still attending school, and, secondly, that it should be seen as a staging post for returning to school, or moving on to college or work-based learning, such as an apprenticeship.

After the Act was passed and the name change agreed, the government ran a consultation on draft statutory guidance, which ended in March 2010, with the rather lengthy title, *Statutory Guidance for Local Authorities and Schools on Information Passports, Personal Learning Plans and the Core Entitlement for all Pupils in Pupil Referral Units and other Alternative Provision* (DCSF, 2009).The title itself makes it clear that all forms of alternative provision, including short stay schools, will be required to give all pupils:

- *Information Passports* for all those who are in alternative provision for at least five days and which bring together previous information about them and go with them to their next destination
- *Personal Learning Plans* for those who are in alternative provision for at least ten days, identifying their educational needs, their targets and intended destination
- *a Core Entitlement* to full-time education which includes English, maths, scientific literacy, ICT, and personal and social development, plus careers advice for secondary pupils. Support must be available from educational psychologists (EPs), Child and Adolescent Mental Health Services (CAMHS), and from social workers as required.

Short stay schools can offer education directly, or they can arrange packages that involve some of the external providers listed previously under Alternative Provision. Many short stay schools also work with mainstream schools to support vulnerable pupils and those at risk of exclusion. They may do this through outreach support to pupils within the schools, or by dual registration, whereby a pupil stays on the register of his or her school, but is also registered with, and attends, the short-stay provision.

Dacorum Education Support Centre

Although the name change applies in law, former PRUs will continue to be free to use any name they wish. Hertfordshire, for instance, has always called its PRUs Education Support Centres (ESCs) and plans to continue to do so. The Dacorum Education Support Centre caters for secondary-aged students. Key stage 3 students are based at the Centre, while key stage 4 students have their own suite of rooms at a nearby college. The head teacher, Rena Cooksley-Harris, says that she would describe many of her students as disaffected rather than having behaviour, emotional or social difficulties (BESD). She says that the answer to getting them re-engaged in the learning process is to offer them an education designed to meet their needs and appeal to their interests. She believes strongly that taking a personalised approach can turn around the disaffected and this is what the Centre aims to do.

 Case study: Dacorum Education Support Centre (DESC)

Situated in Hemel Hempstead, DESC educates up to 55 pupils at any one time. The aim of the DESC is to re-engage students who are disaffected with learning, so that they can return to school or move on successfully to a college or work placement.

Key stage 3

The Centre works closely with local schools through behaviour and attendance partnerships and other more informal contacts. It encourages schools to allow pupils to transfer to the Centre rather than having to be excluded first. For those who are likely to benefit from a short programme of support, there is a six-week re-engagement programme, whereby students attend the Centre and are followed up by the outreach teacher when they return to school. As part of this programme, the Centre runs behaviour surgeries for secondary school staff, as well as for parents and carers, so that adults both at home and at school have a better understanding of how to support the young people.

Key stage 4

For students based at the local college, there are three routes they can take. They can follow GCSE courses, take vocational courses or have an individualised programme. For those taking the GCSE route, the majority of students

(Continued)

(Continued)

move from having below-average attainment on entry to broadly average results at GCSE. Other qualifications include NVQs, BTech Diplomas, Unit Awards, Entry Level Certificates and Bronze and Silver Youth Awards. Students are taught to be resilient and to regard any setbacks, such as having to leave a work placement, not as a failure, but as an opportunity to learn from the experience. One of the slogans used with the college students is: 'Come with a past; leave with a future', which is a reminder to the students themselves and to the staff who work with them, that although the past cannot be altered, the future is up to them.

The outreach service

Although younger pupils do not attend the Centre, the outreach service provides early intervention support to local schools from the foundation stage through to key stage 4. It also ensures a smooth transition for students who are reintegrating. Each has a Passport back to school, so that learning can continue without a break. The Service is flexible enough to run a series of preventative programmes as the need arises. For instance, having identified a lack of parental support could put primary pupils at risk, Family Learning Groups were started. Another scheme focused on looking at friendship groups with groups of girls who were always arguing and falling out with each other. By discussing their behaviour records, they were able to gain an insight into how they were behaving and the effect this had on others. Through these discussions, over time they were able to modify their behaviour and improve their ability to relate to others.

The way the students behave while at the Centre is usually quite different to the behaviour that led to them being removed from their previous environment. As the head teacher says, the proof of the Centre's success is the fact that hardly any students become NEETs (Not in Education, Employment or Training). The Centre is already working along the lines suggested by the draft guidance. It has always seen its role as running short-term provision and, from the time they arrive, there is a plan leading towards the students' next stage of learning and a Passport to take with them on the journey. In Chapter 6 (Figure 6.3), there is an example of the Centre's approach to working in partnership with students and their families. It shows the six-stage procedure involved in the transition of a student to the Centre, which has been found to be particularly important in the transfer of the most disaffected students.

Greys Education Centre, Bedfordshire

A different approach is taken in Bedfordshire, where personalised learning is delivered through e-learning. Five years ago, Greys Education Centre started to offer an e-learning provision, so that pupils who were not in school could have access to a Virtual Learning Environment (VLE) at all times. Two of the drivers for taking this approach were the government's strategy paper

Harnessing technology: Transforming Learning and Children's Services (DfES, 2005c) and Christine Gilbert's *2020 Vision: Report of the Teaching and Learning in 2020 Review Group* (DfES, 2006b), which has been mentioned previously. Both these documents recommend the use of ICT to support pupils' learning and to provide access from home as well as at school.

 Key points: Virtual Learning Environments (VLEs) and learning platforms

VLEs started to appear in schools at the turn of the century. They are designed to assist in classroom learning as well as being able to support distance learners to gain remote access to materials. More recently, the term *learning platforms* is being used. These have administrative functions as well. Learning platforms consist of a collection of hardware and software to support teaching, learning, management and administration. Their many uses include:

- pupils being able to access information at all times and wherever they are
- teachers being able to share their lesson planning and recording of assessments
- parents being able to keep up to date with what their children are learning and the progress they are making
- schools being able to record attendance, timetabling and management information.

In addition, they enable pupils, parents and staff to talk to each other and to access information.

In January 2009, Ofsted, in its report, *Virtual Learning Environments: An Evaluation of Their Development in a Sample of Educational Settings*, looked at what progress had been made in introducing VLEs and found that where they existed, their use was not being fully exploited. Pupils should have had access to a personalised online learning space since 2008 and by 2010 every school should have integrated learning and management systems.

Despite Bedfordshire's recent split into unitary authorities (Bedford Borough Council and Central Bedfordshire Council), it was decided to keep Greys Education Centre for the whole of the county (excluding Luton, which has been a unitary authority for many years).

Case study: Greys Education Centre, Bedfordshire

Greys Education Centre operates as a PRU/short stay school. It is used to meet the needs of pupils who are permanently excluded, students with medical

(Continued)

(Continued)

needs, pregnant schoolgirls and other vulnerable groups. The Centre has several locations. There are separate sites for Middle Years, Years 9 and 10, and Year 11.

The e-learning provision is offered to key stage 4 students from all the upper schools in the county. (Bedfordshire has had a three-tier system of schooling.) It is designed to give students, parents and schools access to a VLE so that:

- those who are on the roll of the Centre have access to a learning platform at all times
- personalised learning is facilitated and can be tailored to students' interests
- students can communicate with teachers and peer mentors who have been trained to support them
- students can become re-engaged and follow nationally accredited courses.

Staff at the Centre have measured the impact of e-learning on the students. Qualitative evidence suggests that they find e-learning motivating, as it allows them to follow their interests, work at their own pace and have some control over where and when learning takes place. One student said that she studied at night when she was bored. Other evidence points to improved results, including at GCSE, with 30% of the 2008 cohort achieving five A*–C grades and over 64% five A*–G grades, in line with the national average.

The head of Greys Education Centre, Terry Ashmore, says: 'Being excluded from school can have a devastating effect on a child's life unless they have access to high quality learning whenever and wherever they want to learn'. Rashida Din, who oversees the e-learning side of the Centre's work, stresses the importance of a partnership approach with schools, and with students and their families. An outline of this approach in the context of e-learning is given as a photocopiable resource in Chapter 6 (Figure 6.5).

Questions for reflection

1. Do you think primary schools should be included in behaviour and attendance partnerships as a matter of course?
2. How many different kinds of alternative provision are you aware of that pupils in your area can access?
3. What have you found to be the most useful developments in technology as far as the education of pupils with SEND is concerned?
4. Do you think there is an overlap between the work of short stay schools and special schools? If so, how do you think this should be resolved?

In the same way that the previous chapter saw specialist schools raising standards in neighbouring schools, co-located and federated schools may be seen as a means of helping to improve outcomes for pupils in schools other than their own. Similarly, students who do not respond well to being in an ordinary school, may gain a new interest in learning if removed to a different environment.

 Summary

This chapter considered some of the ways in which groups of schools are working together through being co-located and/or federated, so that their facilities, resources and expertise can be combined. This can be seen as benefiting all pupils and of being particularly helpful to pupils with SEND. Examples were given of co-located schools, a school co-located with other services and three schools that are both federated and co-located under one roof and one school leader.

Short stay schools and other forms of alternative provision were discussed and case studies provided of two very different approaches, both of which have been the means of reconnecting students with learning and giving them the motivation to succeed.

Further reading

Department for Children, Schools and Families (2008) *Back on Track: A Strategy for Modernising Alternative Provision for Young People.* Available at www.teachernet.gov.uk/publications
Department for Children, Schools and Families (2009) *Learning Behaviour: Lessons Learned.* Nottingham: DCSF Publications.
Knight, S. (2009) *Forest Schools and Outdoor Learning in the Early Years.* London: Sage.
Ofsted (2009) *Virtual Learning Environments: An Evaluation of Their Development in a Sample of Educational Settings.* Available at www.ofsted.gov.uk

Schools working in partnership with other organisations

> This chapter moves from how schools are working collaboratively with each other, to consider some of the partnerships schools are forming with a range of outside organisations.
>   Case studies are given of:
>
> - an academy whose innovative approach to the curriculum helps it to provide for students with a wide range of needs
> - a mainstream school and a special school that each have Trust status
> - a special school in Wales that has formed a business link to develop accredited awards for students who have learning difficulties.

The previous chapter looked at how partnership working between groups of schools has become established, through forming links for specific purposes, or by becoming co-located or federated. This chapter moves beyond groups of schools working together, to look at the wider partnerships schools are forming, both with other educational providers and with a range of organisations that lie outside the usual educational circles. To illustrate this development, the chapter considers the creation of academies, and, more recently, of trust schools. These schools work with a range of sponsors and partners, such as further and higher education (FE and HE), businesses, charities and voluntary organisations. Case studies are given of an academy and two trust schools, as well as a school in Wales that has formed a partnership with a local business in order to develop and market awards for students with SEND.

Academies

As described in the introductory chapter, academies are referred to as state-funded independent schools, which are sponsored by different organisations. They are not part of the local authority (LA), but report directly to the Department for Education (DfE). They are all-ability schools. Newer academies have fewer freedoms than those that were established early on. They may be sponsored by universities, educational trusts, charities, businesses or faith communities. Sponsors may run a chain of academies or be responsible for a single institution. Like City Technology Colleges (CTC), it was envisaged that they would serve inner-city areas and so, to start with, they were called City Academies, but it was later realised that there are pockets of deprivation in other areas as well as inner cities and the word 'City' was dropped from the title.

By 2002, the first three academies were established. Originally, schools had to raise £2 million towards becoming an academy, which they did with the help of outside sponsors. However, in an attempt to get more universities, high-performing colleges and schools interested in running academies, since the autumn of 2007, this requirement has been waived for these groups. Like specialist schools, academies have a specialism in one or more areas of the curriculum.

One of the first steps taken by the Coalition Government was an Academies Act, opening up academy status to primary schools from September 2010 and special schools from September 2011.

Responsibility for academies

Until recently, the academies programme was managed by the DCSF, which funded the academies directly, as LAs are not involved. This changed in April 2010, when responsibility for the funding and provision of the education and training of post-16 learners moved back from the Learning and Skills Council (LSC) to LAs. At the same time, the Young People's Learning Agency (YPLA) and the Skills Funding Agency (SFA) were formed.

 Key points: Responsibility for post-16 provision

Learning and Skills Council (LSC)

The LSC was formed in 2001, but under the Apprenticeships, Skills, Children and Learning Act (DCSF, 2009e), responsibility for planning and funding post-16 provision returned to LAs. For learners with a learning difficulty or disability (LLDD), this duty covers the 19–25 age range.

Young People's Learning Agency (YPLA)

At the same time as the demise of the LSC, the Young People's Learning Agency (YPLA) was established to support LAs in planning and commissioning the provision of education and training for young people. In addition, the YPLA was given the function of funding and performance managing the academies while the DCSF continued to commission and open new academies. This arrangement may or may not continue under the present government.

Skills Funding Agency (SFA)

The SFA was created at the same time as the YPLA with a remit to distribute funding for post-19 learners in colleges of further education.

These changes occurred at the same time as legislation to ensure the raising of the participation age to 17 years of age by 2013 and to 18 years of age by 2015. This has commonly been referred to as raising the school leaving age, but young people will not have to stay in school beyond 16. Instead, they will be able to choose between being in full-time education at a school or college, engaged in work-based learning, such as an apprenticeship scheme, or if they are employed, combining work with part-time education or training. As participation post-16 is voluntary at present, it is hoped that this will reduce the number of 'NEETS' (not in employment, education or training), as well as enhancing the skills of the workforce. The range of opportunities available at post-16 is extending all the time. There are more apprenticeship schemes available, the full range of the 14–19 diplomas is coming on stream and there is Foundation Learning for students below GCSE standard.

All-through schools

At present, most academies are secondary schools, although a few are all-age schools. By the end of 2009, there were 14 all-through academies, with some going from nursery to 19 years of age. The Consortium of All Through Schooling (CATS) is the national interest group and it has members from all-through schools and academies, all-through federations, all-through trusts, as well as from LAs and individual consultants. Most all-through schools retain separate primary and secondary buildings. Merged and federated schools are the most common model for all-age schools. All-through educational models were seen as a key part of the last government's strategy for raising attainment and improving outcomes for children.

 Key points: The Consortium of All Through Schooling (CATS)

The full title for CATS is The National Consortium for All-through Schools, Federations and Learning Communities. It is a not-for-profit limited company funded by member subscriptions. CATS has been supported by the Department for Children, Schools and Families (DCSF), the Specialist Schools and Academies Trust (SSAT) and the Innovation Unit. It offers support to schools and local authorities, through its consultancy arm, as they develop their plans for future all-through schooling structures.

The appointment in 2006 of Sir Bruce Liddington as the first Schools Commissioner, was largely to assist the move to these newer types of schools, and, in particular, as a way of moving forward the national challenge schools, some of which have been turned into academies.

National challenge schools

The National Challenge programme was launched in June 2008, with the aim of raising results by tackling underachievement in secondary schools.

The secretary of state at the time, Ed Balls, explained that this programme was the next phase of the government's school improvement strategy. In *The Children's Plan* (2007), a goal was set for 90% or more of pupils to achieve the equivalent of five good GCSEs by the year 2020. The National Challenge programme targets secondary schools where less than 30% of students achieve this. Additional money has been targeted at the schools, which have been encouraged to consider being converted into academies, or forming partnerships with other schools through being federated or becoming trust schools.

 Key points: National challenge schools

National Challenge is the government programme to ensure that every maintained secondary school, including academies, has at least 30% of their pupils achieving five good (A* to C) GCSEs by 2011. To reach this figure, the London Challenge programme has been extended nationally. Strategies include extra funding for schools to buy in additional expertise, linking a strong school with a weaker one, or the school becoming an academy, a trust school or joining a federation.

While no one would dispute the need to raise standards and to ensure that all pupils, whatever their background or difficulties in learning, have every opportunity to achieve their potential, the National Challenge programme has been seen by some schools as singling them out unfairly. Schools vary enormously in their pupil populations, and, within schools, year groups vary, so that schools do not necessarily see a year-on-year increase in results. Some have welcomed the additional funding and extra support that national challenge schools receive, while others have felt that being in the public eye in this way has had a detrimental effect, preventing them from attracting the very pupils who might help to raise their results.

 Questions for reflection

1. Do you think the creation of academies has improved the educational opportunities for some pupils?
2. What do you see as the value of all-through schools and what forms do you think they should take?
3. Do you think there is a danger of confusing underachievement with SEND?

The Hereford Academy

The first case study in this chapter is of The Hereford Academy, which has made a point of raising standards through making the curriculum more accessible to all its students. Much of its intervention work is based on the

'5Rs' given below, which build on the ones identified by the psychologist, Guy Claxton, in his book, *Building Learning Power: Helping Young People to Become Better Learners* (2002). Rather than the '3Rs' of old, Claxton's work concentrates on the four attributes he thinks today's students need, which he calls resilience, resourcefulness, reflectiveness and reciprocity, with the latter meaning the ability to work with others as well as by oneself. The first three of Claxton's terms are used by The Hereford Academy. 'Reciprocity' is replaced by 'relationships' and Hereford has added 'readiness' as a fifth 'R'. It is significant that these concepts are seen as applicable to both students and to the staff who work with them.

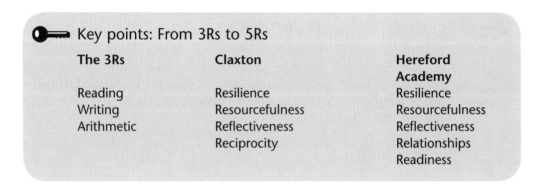

	Key points: From 3Rs to 5Rs	
The 3Rs	**Claxton**	**Hereford Academy**
Reading	Resilience	Resilience
Writing	Resourcefulness	Resourcefulness
Arithmetic	Reflectiveness	Reflectiveness
	Reciprocity	Relationships
		Readiness

In September 2006, the Hereford Diocese agreed to sponsor The Hereford Academy, to replace Wyebridge Sports College. The Academy opened in September 2008 and the construction of the new buildings began the following year. These are due to be completed in 2011. Wyebridge Sports College closed formally on 31 August 2008 and opened as The Hereford Academy on 1 September 2008. The school serves the same area it has done in the past.

The Hereford Academy has kept its former specialism in Sport and added Science and Health as additional specialisms. As well as its sponsor, the Academy has a number of partners which include: the University of Worcester and the University of Gloucester; the South Wye Regeneration Project, which focuses on creating employment opportunities and having a better trained workforce, and Peter Prosser Hairdressing Ltd, which is a government-approved training centre for hairdressing. Between them, these partners (and others who have joined more recently), increase the opportunities offered to the whole range of students by providing valuable links into the worlds of higher education (HE) and employment.

 Case study: The Hereford Academy

The Academy has around 800 students, but will increase to 900 when the new building is ready. Two years ago, it added a sixth form, so that it is able to take students aged 11–19. The Academy is situated in the most disadvantaged area of Hereford. As it wanted to develop a new approach to the curriculum that would give access to all students, including the high percentage of those who have SEND and other additional needs, The Academy runs four different types of curriculum based on stages of learning. These are:

- Transitional
- Progress
- Customised
- Enhanced.

Within each of these, there are three different pathways, so that students can work at different speeds:

- Accelerated Learners
- Breakthrough Learners
- Tailored Learning.

In order to avoid changing the structure of the curriculum too quickly, the changes were brought in first with Year 7 and will not be fully operational until the new building is completed. For the present, a Learning Zone, where intervention work takes place, has been created out of four temporary classrooms. Support starts from before a child leaves primary school, and pupils who are seen as vulnerable are given the opportunity to spend time at the academy before they transfer. Their needs are assessed and intervention programmes are put in place before they arrive.

Regardless of age, students requiring additional support are divided into three levels of need: olympic standard, for those who need the most intensive intervention programmes, followed by gold standard for the middle group of students and silver standard for those who still need an intervention programme, but one that is less intensive and may not be needed in the longer term. Detailed provision mapping shows the targets students are expected to reach at the end of each intervention programme, as well as how its impact will be measured. Recently, support for those where attendance or behaviour is problematic has been brought under the staff in the Learning Zone.

As well as teaching staff, there are 20 learning support workers (LSWs) attached to the Learning Zone, who work with individual pupils in class, assist with intervention groups and support across all subject areas, including vocational subjects. The continuing professional development (CPD) of LSWs is seen as being as important as that of the teachers and Chris Atkinson, the special educational needs coordinator (SENCO), seeks to ensure that all her staff have the relevant expertise to fulfil their various roles.

The Principal, John Sheppard, and his staff have been closely involved with the design of the new building and have been able to try to create an environment that will embody the personalised approach to learning that the school has developed. There will be spaces for individual and small group work, plus flexible learning spaces that can be used to accommodate different sized classes. Instead of traditional corridors, space is being allowed for students to move around more easily and to give them pleasant areas for socialising out of lesson time. Although the Academy's new building will further enhance the school's ability to personalise the curriculum, its innovative approach is already being reflected in the school's results and reputation.

While the Principal believes that school leaders who have a clear sense of purpose and a vision for their school, will always seek to be innovative, he believes that being an academy has given him greater freedom to be able to move the school in the direction he feels it needs to take, as well as giving him the opportunity to create an environment that is designed to meet the needs of all the students, providing them with the skills they will need in their future lives.

In Charles Leadbetter's (2008) book, *What's Next? 21 Ideas for 21st Century Learning*, he sees relationships as central to learning. His expression that 'Learning is best done with people rather than to or for them', is very much the approach of The Hereford Academy. There is a strong feeling of partnership between the staff and students in the Learning Zone, which may stem partly from the fact that they both see themselves as learners who are engaged in developing the attributes highlighted by the 5Rs of resourcefulness, resilience, readiness, reflectiveness and relationships. In Chapter 6 (Figure 6.2a), there is an example of the pro forma used by the Academy for pupils' personal targets in Literacy, which are grouped under the headings of the 5Rs, as well as a similar approach to using a Pupil Self-Assessment Questionnaire (Figure 6.2b).

Trust schools

While specialist school status is only open to schools with secondary-aged pupils and the academies programme has been largely for secondary schools, becoming a trust school is open to primary, secondary and special schools. Trusts may support a single school or a group of schools. If the latter, an overarching trust will be formed and all the schools within it will be described as trust schools. Trust schools are different from academies in that they remain within the LA, but they are similar in drawing on additional expertise as a way of delivering higher standards, including colleges and universities, as well as the commercial and voluntary sectors.

Any maintained school can become a trust school if the governing body opts to go down this route. However, if the school is not a foundation school already, it must become a foundation school before becoming a trust school. The Education and Inspections Act 2006 included the provision for a foundation school to set up a charitable foundation (or trust) to support the school. In other words, existing foundation schools can set up a charitable trust in order to become trust schools, while community schools take on foundation status and set up a trust within a single process. (The difference between community and foundation schools was discussed in the introductory chapter.) There are five steps to becoming a trust school:

1. The governing body decides it wants to take this step and who its partners will be.
2. The schools consults those who would be affected by the change, including parents, staff, trade unions and the local community.
3. The school publishes details of who is on the Trust.
4. After considering the responses to its proposals, the governing body decides whether or not to go ahead.

5. If it goes ahead with Trust status, the school's land and buildings are transferred to the Trust.

 Key points: Academies and trust schools

Academies

Academies have existed since 2000 and are independent of the LA. The governing body or the sponsoring Trust appoints the school staff and acts as the employer.

Trust schools

Trust schools were created by the Education and Inspections Act of 2006. They are state-funded foundation schools supported by a charitable trust. They manage their own assets and employ their own staff. A majority of the governing body can be appointed by the Trust, in which case a parent council must be established as well. A Trust may consist of one or more schools.

Both academies and trust schools have close ties with a range of organisations. For academies, these will be its sponsors and it may have other partners. For trust schools, the organisations will be its partners.

Trust schools can also be formed as the result of a competition for a new school. Under the 2006 Education and Inspections Act, whereby LAs became the commissioners of services rather than the providers, other prospective providers must be invited to put in a proposal for a new school. This does not apply if an existing school is being rebuilt on the same site, the school is for 16–19-year-olds or the LA is working with a sponsor to establish an academy.

South Dartmoor Community College

An example of a school that has become a trust school is South Dartmoor Community College in Devon, which has been a Specialist Sports College since 1997, a training school since 2001 and a trust school since 2007. Becoming a training school is one of the options open to schools that are already High Performing Specialist Schools.

 Case study: South Dartmoor Community College

South Dartmoor is a comprehensive school for 1670 students aged 11–18. It is large for a school in a rural setting. As well as being a Specialist Sports College and a training school, since 2009, it has been a School of Creativity, joining a network of schools finding innovative ways of delivering teaching and learning, and influencing developments locally and nationally.

(Continued)

(Continued)

When the possibility of pursuing trust status was first explored, there were several secondary schools in the county that were interested and the initial thinking was that they might become part of one trust. However, when discussing this option in more detail, it became clear that the schools had different ideas about how they wanted to develop and the partners they wanted to include, so South Dartmoor become a trust school on its own. The LA has supported its schools in taking this route and the school continues to maintain links and to draw on the LA's services.

The four organisations that make up the Trust are varied and each brings different expertise to the role. They are:

- *Exeter University School of Education,* which has made joint appointments with the school, so that teachers can work across both organisations. They also work together on researching aspects of teaching and learning, including how to improve outcomes for students with SEND.
- *Capita Children's Services,* which has worked with the school for some time and is using the connection to try out new software for refining data analysis at national level, and helps train parents to bring the school into the home electronically.
- *TLO,* an educational publishing company which promotes 'Building Learning Power'. TLO has a role in helping develop independent learning and student voice.
- *E. & J.W. Glendinning Ltd,* which is a local firm providing quarry and concrete products. The firm has worked on building projects with the school in the past and continues to support the school in developing its facilities, in particular in improving provision for sports.

Ray Tarleton, the Principal, sees giving businesses, charities and higher education a voice in education through being involved with trust schools, a positive move forward, widening the education debate and the expertise available to schools. He says: 'I believe that schools need to look outwards and draw in the skills and talents in this way, so the concept is one I fully support.'

As well as involving outside organisations through its trust status, South Dartmoor has sought to raise standards and simplify information sharing by introducing a *learning gateway.* This enables people to have a single point from which they can access information from different systems. In a school situation, it is a way of giving teachers, students and parents access to a range of information and to communicate in a number of different ways. Some information can be freely shared by all concerned while other information will only be available to certain groups. At South Dartmoor, the learning gateway was built around the needs of teaching staff first, then students and lastly parents. As well as enabling teachers and students to keep in touch, it means parents can keep track of their children's progress and know what they are learning. Peter Kensington, the Assistant Principal and Director of Assessment and Technologies, who built up the system from a commercial package, has found out by trial and error the best way of approaching the task. His 'Top Tips' are featured in Chapter 6 (Figure 6.4). He says there is evidence that some of the parents who previously did not take a close interest in their children's education have become more engaged and that this has encouraged, in particular, students who were underperforming.

The St Christopher School in Leigh-on-Sea

The St Christopher School in Leigh-on-Sea opened in 1906 and was one of a very few special schools to have been a grant maintained (GM) school before becoming a foundation school in 1999.

 Key points: Grant maintained schools

Grant maintained status came in with the 1988 Education Reform Act, which also heralded the national curriculum, local management of schools (LMS) and Ofsted. It was part of the drive by a Conservative government to create a greater diversity of schools and to decrease the power of LAs. GM schools were managed and owned by their governing bodies.

Under the 1993 Education Act, Independent schools were able to become GM schools and enter the state system. At their peak, there were over 1000 GM schools, representing 19% of secondary schools, 3% of primary schools and 2% of special schools.

GM status was abolished by the School Standards and Framework Act of 1998, leaving the 15 CTCs as the only schools directly funded by the government, until the emergence of city academies (later academies) in 2000.

In 2006, The St Christopher School became a specialist school for communication and interaction. The following year, it made the move from being a foundation school to having trust status. This means that it is officially described as a Specialist Foundation Trust Special School.

 Case study: The St Christopher Foundation Special School (a SEN Specialist School for Communication and Interaction)

The school has increased substantially in size and caters for 185 pupils aged 3–19. In 2005, when the unitary authority of Southend-on-Sea reorganised its special schools, The St Christopher School became a school for primary-aged pupils with a range of learning difficulties, but with provision for pupils on the autism spectrum and/or those with attention deficit hyperactivity disorder (ADHD) to stay on for their secondary education. Since 2008, it has had provision for 16–19-year-olds as well. On the same site is

(Continued)

(Continued)

Christopher's Cottage, which provides all-year-round respite care for a small number of children at a time from the area.

The Trust, which is known as The St Christopher Young People's Trust, has been set up with a focus on autism (including Asperger's syndrome) and ADHD. It seeks to heighten people's understanding of these conditions and to work to increase opportunities for them within the local community. Members of the Trust are:

- The St Christopher School
- Prospects Learning Foundation (an educational charity that runs Prospects College. The college has a wide range of vocational courses)
- South East Essex College
- Southend Mencap (Mencap being the leading UK charity for people with learning disabilities and their families)
- Supporting Aspergers Families in Essex (SAFE)
- community representatives.

The majority of governors on the Trust are school governors, so the school does not have a Parent Council as well. The Trust has raised funds for some joint posts, including a Family Support Worker, and has put on two conferences to raise awareness of autism and ADHD.

The head teacher, Jackie Mullan, says that the benefits of having trust status is not so much about attracting extra funding, as making sure the school looks outwards to the local community, helping people to understand the nature of the difficulties young people can have and increasing the provision and opportunities open to them once they leave school.

The St Christopher School's work as a trust school ties in with its communication and interaction specialism. This allowed the school to build a Communication and Interaction Centre, which, again, is used to improve people's understanding of these difficulties. As well as providing a welcoming area for specialist support groups, including SAFE and ADHD United to meet, there are training facilities which are used by a wide variety of professionals, including trainees from the police force, early years degree students, social workers and nurses. Part of the training for these groups involves spending time in the classes, so that they can gain a better understanding of the needs of the children and young people at the school.

Schools working with other organisations

The Labour Government encouraged links between schools and other organisations, including businesses. In 2007, the Prime Minister at the time set up the National Council for Educational Excellence (NCEE), to look at how businesses and universities might work with schools and colleges to raise standards. It also looked at how successful schools and colleges might share their expertise to support others. In 2008, the DCSF produced *Building*

Stronger Partnerships (2008h). Read one way up, the document is entitled *Schools, Colleges, Children's and Families' Services: How Employers Can Support You.* When the document is reversed, it reads, *Employers: How You Can Support Schools, Colleges, Children and Families.* The publication gives examples and ideas for how schools and other organisations can interact for the benefit of students.

The links that schools form as part of being an academy or a trust school have already been discussed. Some schools that do not fall into these categories have also been entrepreneurial in building up links with outside organisations. In Wales, for instance, where academies and trust schools do not exist as an option, schools have sought to develop their own partnerships with outside agencies.

Woodlands High School, Cardiff

Woodlands is a secondary school for students with a range of learning difficulties, that has established a partnership with Primus Training and Consultancy Company. Through working with relevant organisations, the school has developed accredited courses for students who are below GCSE level, which Primus Training has helped to market and produce. The courses have been accredited by Education and Development International (EDI), which accredits vocational and professional qualifications in the UK and internationally.

 Case study: Woodlands High School, Cardiff

Woodlands is a special school for 130 students aged 11–19. It caters for a range of learning difficulties from moderate to severe (MLD and SLD). Students who have profound and multiple learning difficulties (PMLD) have provision in a different school.

A small minority of students take one or more GCSEs, but most need courses below this level. Having explored various options, the school felt that it wanted to produce courses that would meet the needs of this group of students, which would also be seen as worthwhile by local businesses. The school had an informal partnership with Primus Training, who first became involved through sponsoring the school for some events and then became one of the school's business links for students on work experience.

Over the course of three years, Lisa Purcell, the school's careers teacher, worked with the Founder and Director of Primus Training, Sean Colsey, to develop and market a series of courses that would suit students who are capable of gaining worthwhile awards, but at a level below that of GCSE. To make sure the courses would deliver the skills businesses wanted, each course has been developed in conjunction with relevant organisations. Six courses have now been published. They combine students' interests with the skills businesses require, leading to better prospects for work placements and job opportunities.

(Continued)

(Continued)

The scheme is called Moving On Up and the courses developed so far are:

- Introduction to ICT skills
- Office Skills (in conjunction with the Welsh Assembly Government)
- Garden and Park Skills
- Basic Work Skills (in conjunction with Cardiff Council Works Department)
- Customer Care
- Café and Restaurant Skills (in conjunction with Cardiff Council).

The courses are designed to run alongside relevant and tailored work experience placements. Students work through them at their own pace. Further courses are in development. Schools in both Wales and England have shown an interest in the scheme and have started to purchase it.

The head teacher, Russell Webb, says the scheme has led to more offers of work placements and, in some cases, to employment. He would like students to have the option of staying on until 25 years of age, so that they are given more time to develop the skills they need to gain permanent employment. In Chapter 6 (Figure 6.8), there is a flowchart showing those involved in developing Moving On Up.

 Summary

This chapter has covered the development of two newer types of schools – academies and trust schools – as well as an example of a school in Wales that has been entrepreneurial in working with local businesses to extend the courses available to students with learning difficulties.

All the case studies show that forging links with a wider group of organisations has enabled the schools concerned to provide more resources and wider opportunities for their own pupils, as well as ensuring that the schools are outward looking and forward thinking.

Further reading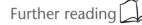

Claxton, G. (2002) *Building Learning Power: Helping Young People to Become Better Learners*. Bristol: TLO.

Department for Children, Schools and Families (2008) *Building Stronger Partnerships*. Available at www.teachernet.gov.uk/publications

Leadbetter, C. (2008) *What's Next? 21 Ideas for 21st Century Learning*. London: The Innovation Unit.

Smith, A. (2009) *Learning to Learn in Practice: The L2 Approach*. Carmarthen: Crown House.

5

Schools working in partnership with other services

This chapter moves from looking at schools that have the support of sponsors and other partners from the world of business and elsewhere, to considering the development of partnership working between education, health and social care, as exemplified through the work of:

- an extended primary school with a children's centre
- a non-maintained school with a children's centre
- a local authority's Integrated Disability Service
- a charity working with a local authority (LA).

The four case studies illustrate different ways in which the closer integration of services is having a positive effect on children from less advantaged backgrounds and those who have special educational needs and disabilities (SEND).

This chapter contains the remaining case studies and concentrates on schools and services that have formed close working relationships with health and social care. As explained in the introductory chapter, when the *Every Child Matters* green paper (DfES, 2003) and the Children Act of 2004, led to local education authorities (LAs) becoming part of children's services departments, this was seen as being particularly beneficial to vulnerable children and families, including those with SEND. For this is the group that is more likely to draw on at least two of the three public services and, in many cases, all three, as well as a range of other organisations, including the voluntary sector. Pupils with SEND may have medical needs, and many will need the support of a range of therapists who work for the health service, such as speech and language therapists (SaLTs), occupational therapists or physiotherapists. In addition, social care may be needed to provide respite for families labouring under the additional strain of caring for a child with SEND, as well as social workers supporting children and families in a number of ways.

This chapter looks at how this closer working between the services, at both school and local authority level, is improving the support to pupils and their families. Examples are given of schools that run children's centres and those that are extended schools. The expectations on schools are tremendous and can only be achieved by schools working in partnership with each other and with other services and providers. LAs have a role in making sure all schools, including special schools, are part of extended schools' consortia or clusters, so that access to services can be provided in each area. In addition, they need to ensure that the aim of having one children's centre for every community will be achieved, if this remains the aim of the Coalition Government.

Children's centres and extended schools

To some extent, children's centres and extended schools are part of the same package, but have often been treated as separate entities. This may have arisen because, while every school is expected to become an extended school, not every school will have a children's centre. Many children's centres are attached to other providers or operate from separate buildings. Like extended schools, they vary in what they provide, depending on the needs of the area and the level of demand for particular activities.

Extended schools

When the concept of schools becoming extended schools was first mooted, it seemed, at first glance, to be a new, and not necessarily very welcome, idea on the part of schools, who were concerned about the added workload and having to switch the focus of their attention from teaching and learning to a whole raft of other activities, involving whole families and even whole communities. In fact, the concept was not entirely new, as schools had been used to offering a variety of out-of-school activities, including team practices and matches against other schools and a range of other events. As early as the 1920s, the Cambridgeshire village colleges provided activities for rural communities and this idea was later taken up in other parts of the country. Boarding schools have always provided activities for their pupils beyond the school day, although not necessarily for the community as well. Another forerunner was the out-of-school-hours learning (OSHL) or study support programmes. What was new about the extended schools approach was the notion that it would involve every school. For many, this was a very significant shift from focusing all their energies on what happened to their pupils during the school day, to thinking in terms of being open for longer hours, for more days in the year, providing for families as well as for pupils and making their facilities available to the local community.

By 2010, all schools were expected to be part of the move towards extended schooling. This does not mean that every school must provide the core offer, but that every school will be able to signpost families and the community to where the various parts of the core offer are available. Every LA is expected to have an Extended Schools Remodelling Adviser (ESRA), who is supported by the Training and Development Agency for schools (TDA). In most areas, clusters of schools work together in Extended School Partnerships. Most schools have their own extended schools coordinators, who act as a link with other schools, as well as overseeing the development of their own school's work in this area.

The core offer of services the government expects schools to offer, in partnership with LAs and with the private and voluntary sectors, is as follows:

- a varied menu of activities, combined with childcare in primary schools, from 8am to 6pm, for five days a week and for 48 weeks a year
- parenting support, including parenting programmes and family learning sessions
- community access to the school's facilities for adult learning
- swift and easy access to targeted and specialist services.

This last heading includes improving the early identification of SEND and of others who have additional needs, so that support can be arranged as soon as possible. Providing easier access to all types of services around the places where children and young people spend most of their time, is seen as key to meeting the five objectives of ECM. These are that children are healthy, stay safe, enjoy and achieve, make a positive contribution and achieve economic well-being.

In August 2009, the DCSF commissioned the Thomas Coram Research Unit at the Institute of Education, University of London, to look at inter-professional working in multipurpose children's settings in England and Sweden (Cameron et al., 2009). The researchers identified four types of inter-professional practice:

1. **parallel working**, where agencies are co-located, but little inter-professional work takes place
2. **multi-agency casework**, where agencies work together around individual cases and discuss common concerns, but there may be no co-location or structural change
3. **project teams**, where agencies come together for time-limited purposes and only part of the professionals' time is allocated to integrated working
4. **work groups**, where inter-professional teams engage together throughout the school day, work under a single governance arrangement and take a common and holistic approach to the education and well-being of children.

Whereas Sweden has been used to multi-professional working for longer, the rate of change and its scope has been far broader in England. The study identified some of the facilitators and obstacles to inter-professional activity as follows:

Facilitators

- Commitment
- A willingness to blur professional boundaries

- Good communication and information sharing
- Active involvement
- Leadership
- Clarity about roles and expectations
- Shared aims and objectives

Obstacles

- Complexity of management
- Lack of adequate funding and other resources
- Competing priorities
- Conflicts of interest

Although the report was published in 2009, the study took place between 2006 and 2007. At that time, it suggested that the multi-agency casework approach was the most common of the four in England and that work groups (no. 4) only existed in Sweden. It would be unlikely that the same conclusions would be drawn today. In the foreword to *Extended Schools: Building on Experience* (DCSF, 2007), the Minister for Children, Young People and Families reported that almost half of all schools were well on the way to offering extended services. By the time of publication of *The Children's Plan Two Years On: A Progress Report* (DCSF, 2009b), the figure had risen to 93% of schools offering extended services. While every school has a role to play in developing extended services, schools vary in how closely they are involved with children's centres.

Children's centres

Children's centres have been developed partly around existing provision, such as: maintained nursery schools, primary, secondary and special schools, family centres, community centres, health centres, and voluntary and private provision. Responsibility for early education and childcare in Scotland, Wales and Northern Ireland rests with the separate devolved administrations.

The idea of children's centres grew out of three previous initiatives:

- Early Excellence Centres
- Sure Start
- Neighbourhood Nurseries.

 Key points: The forerunners of children's centres

The Early Excellence Centre Pilot Programme was launched by the government in the late 1990s and over the next two years, 29 pilot EECs were developed, with the aim of having 100 EECs over time. The EECs were designed to operate as one-stop-shops, with different agencies working together to offer integrated care and education services, including early education, daycare, social support and adult learning.

The **Sure Start** programme began in 1998 and was adapted from the American Head Start programme, which had built up evidence that it was effective in improving the life chances of children in areas of high deprivation. Sure Start programmes provided childcare, early education, health and family support. Later, Sure Start became part of the development of children's centres, as set out in the 10-year strategy for childcare (2004).

The **Neighbourhood Nurseries** initiative began in 2000 with the aim of expanding childcare provision to the 20% most disadvantaged areas in England. It was planned to provide some new nurseries and created additional places in existing nurseries. Again, the emphasis was on providing childcare and early learning, so that family members could return to work.

Children's centres have had three phases of development:

Phase 1 – between 2004 and 2006, children's centres were developed to serve families living in the 20% most disadvantaged wards.

Phase 2 – between 2006 and 2008, families in the 30% most disadvantaged areas were targeted and the number of children's centres rose to 2500.

Phase 3 – by 2010, there were due to be 3500 children's centres, so that there would be one to serve every community that has 800 children under five. This target was reached in March 2010.

 Key points: Children's centres and extended schools

Extended schools	Children's centres
A varied menu of activities	Activities for children and parents
	Integrated early learning and childcare with teacher input
Full daycare or childcare in primary schools	Drop-in sessions for children and parents
Parenting support	Support, advice and outreach
Information and advice	Links to Jobcentre Plus and training
Access to targeted and specialist services	Child and family health services
	Support for children and families with SEND
Community access	Support for childminders

N.B. The words in italics relate to additional activities in children's centres in the more deprived areas.

Some children's centres are managed by schools. Although there are more attached to primary schools, both secondary and special schools run children's centres, including a few non-maintained special schools.

This means that in less disadvantaged areas, facilities might include drop-in sessions and some activities for children and their parents or carers, whereas in areas of high disadvantage, there should be integrated childcare and early learning. Although children's centres have existed since the Children Act of 2004, placing them on a statutory basis did not happen until the Apprenticeships, Skills, Children and Learning Act was passed in 2009. This was done in order to put them on a more secure footing.

Children's trusts

Similarly, children's trusts were created by the Children Act of 2004 and put on a statutory footing in the Apprenticeships, Skills, Children and Learning Act (DCSF, 2009e), in order to ensure their long-term future. They are responsible for joint planning and commissioning in order to deliver better services to children and families. The development of children's trusts shows how joint working is becoming part of the fabric of the work of local authorities and their partners.

 Key points: Children's trusts

Children's trusts

Children's trusts bring together all services for children and young people in an area. LAs are the strategic lead, working closely with primary care trusts (PCTs). This opens up the possibility of pooling resources, including budgets.

The Commissioning Support Programme (CSP)

The CSP was launched in the autumn of 2008 to help children's trusts to plan, design and implement services more effectively.

Children's Trust Boards

Trusts are governed by Children's Trust Boards, which have a duty to publish annually a Children and Young People's Plan (CYPP). Schools are one of the key statutory partners and must have a representative on the Board.

 Questions for reflection

1. If you were planning children's centres, where would you try to locate them?
2. What are your views on the benefits and drawbacks of children's centres being managed by schools?
3. Do you see both advantages and disadvantages in schools becoming extended schools?

Goddard Park Community Primary School

The first case study in this chapter is of a primary school that was one of the first schools to manage a children's centre as well as developing the core offer for extended services. Goddard Park is in the unitary authority of Swindon. The head teacher, Mike Welsh, describes his school as a fully integrated primary school, which has provision for babies, as well as activities for adults of all ages, including some who are in their 90s. He is well placed to run an extensive provision, having qualified as a social worker as well as a teacher and then taken the National Professional Qualification in Integrated Centre Leadership (NPQICL).

 Key points: NPQH and NPQICL

National Professional Qualification for Headship (NPQH)

Since April 2009, this has been a mandatory qualification for anyone wishing to be appointed to the headship of a school. The course lasts 4–12 months depending on personal circumstances. At first, it was open to anyone who met the entry requirements and some saw it as useful professional development. However, it is now restricted to those who are actively seeking to become head teachers in the near future.

National Professional Qualification in Integrated Centre Leadership (NPQICL)

The NPQICL was developed to address the needs of leaders within multi-agency and early years settings. The course lasts for a year. It has equivalence with the NPQH. It can also count towards a Masters degree.

Both programmes are run by the National College for Leadership of Schools and Children's Services (formerly known as the National College for School Leaders).

Having previously run a Centre of Early Excellence (EEC), Goddard Park School was in a strong position for this provision to become a Phase 1 Children's Centre. The school is in an area of social deprivation and has an above-average number of children with SEND. One of the approaches used in the early years is Reggio Emilia.

 Key points: Reggio Emilia

This approach to early years education started in a city of that name in Northern Italy after the Second World War. It spread to the USA, New Zealand, Australia and, increasingly, it is being used in the UK. Features include:

- seeing the environment as helping children to learn
- creating a natural environment, using plants, light and wooden, rather than plastic, toys
- forming different spaces to stimulate children's creativity
- believing that children learn through interaction with other people and with the environment.

This approach fits in with the school also being a Forest School, which, again, stresses the importance of the environment in nurturing children's learning. Five years ago, every pupil planted a tree and the area has matured enough for the school to have a trained forest school worker on the staff. (More information about forest schools was given in Chapter 3.)

 Case study: Goddard Park Community Primary School and Integrated Children's Centre

Goddard Park in Swindon started as a primary school, which currently caters for 425 pupils. In addition, it has a children's centre and is a fully extended school. Between them, the children's centre and the extended school provision, which are open for 48 weeks a year from 8am to 6pm, include:

- daycare for 0–5-year-olds, including provision for over 100 babies and toddlers aged six weeks to three years of age
- childcare for children aged 5–11
- nursery provision for 3–5-year-olds
- a varied menu of after-school clubs and other activities
- parenting support and family learning
- access to health services, including health visitors and speech and language therapists
- community access to activities, including a weekly lunch club for senior citizens, which is run by the pupils in Year 5.

In the reception area for the children's centre, a sign on the wall reminds people about the dangers of passive smoking. It reads: **If you smoke, I smoke.**

The primary school, for 4–11-year-olds, provides personalised programmes for pupils who have SEND. These are rigorously monitored through individual learning reviews. Because the staff know most of the pupils and their families from an early stage, support programmes are put in place from the foundation stage upwards. All staff have received additional training in helping pupils who have difficulty acquiring literacy skills. Reading Recovery is used for those who need extra support in Year 1. The school is recognised as a dyslexia-friendly school. Teaching assistants act as mentors for pupils who have behavioural difficulties.

The list of staff shows how the school has taken the opportunity to remodel its workforce to address its extended role. The list includes:

- an extended services coordinator
- three family support workers
- a daycare coordinator
- childcare development workers
- childcare assistants
- two Reading Recovery teachers for Year 1
- a community learning mentor
- playleaders for every age group.

The latter is the title which is used for Midday Supervisory Assistants (MSAs), in order to stress the nature of their role in helping children to have productive playtimes.

As part of encouraging parents and carers to be involved in their children's education, the school provides tutors for adults, so that they can learn alongside their children in class and many who were apprehensive at first, gain the confidence to become parent helpers. Whether or not they help in this way, parents say that they are keener to support their children now that they understand more about what their children are learning and how they can help them. One mother describes herself as someone who was never at school as a child, but now she makes sure her son attends and realises the importance of being at school.

Mike Welsh says he has been running an integrated provision for long enough to be able to see the value, particularly for children from less advantaged backgrounds, who benefit from enriched learning opportunities from an early age. He points to the improvement in key stage results and the increased attendance at clinics, such as speech and language therapy, which has risen from 60% to almost 100% attendance, now that the clinics are held at the school. He is keen to stress, not just the importance of motivating children, but of helping families to want more for their children:

> It is not just about early intervention, but maintaining children's aspirations throughout their time at school. Part of achieving this is to reach out to the families and raising parental aspirations about their children's future.

The second example of a school with a children's centre comes from the non-maintained sector. As explained previously, non-maintained schools are special schools that take children who are paid for by local authorities (LAs), unlike independent schools, where most of the fees are paid by parents who wish their children to attend. Whereas independent schools may or may not be solely for children with SEND, all 70+ non-maintained schools are special schools. These schools must be approved by the secretary of state for education, and not run for profit. Most of these schools are very specialised and cater for children for whom there is no similar provision in the state sector.

A non-maintained school and children's centre – St Piers

St Piers is part of a campus run by The National Centre for Young People with Epilepsy (NCYPE). Established in the 1890s, it was originally a training place where young people with epilepsy could learn how to work and get jobs. Today, the campus houses:

- a medical centre, which is run in conjunction with Great Ormond Street Hospital and the Institute of Child Health, where children can be assessed over a two-day to twelve-week period
- an FE college
- a day and residential school
- a children's home
- a children's centre
- an epilepsy information service

- an outreach and training service for schools, PCTs and others who want to learn more about childhood epilepsy.

There is also a nursery school on the same site, which is not run by the NCYPE.

One in every 200 children has some form of epilepsy, which is the most common severe neurological disorder in the world. In 75% of cases, children either grow out of it or it is kept under control by medication.

Key points: Epilepsy

- An epileptic seizure is the result of a sudden electrical discharge in the brain, which leads to an alteration in the person's sensation, behaviour or consciousness. The nature of a seizure varies depending on its severity and whether the whole, or part, of the brain is affected. There are over 40 different types of seizures or fits, which vary from full or partial consciousness being lost for a matter of seconds to a few minutes.
- *Generalised seizures* affect the whole brain and include tonic–clonic seizures (formerly known as grand mal), where the person loses consciousness completely.
- *Partial seizures* vary and affect different parts of the body, depending on which parts of the brain are affected.

The FE college has around 100 students and is separate from the school, although many pupils will transfer there to complete the next stage of their education. The college has both day and residential students at 16–19 years of age. Students follow a wide variety of courses including ASDAN-accredited courses and some focus on land-based industries using the farm and horticultural centre on the campus. The person-centred approach to education continues and some students will be accompanied to enable them to follow courses at other colleges, or to undertake work experience.

Key points: ASDAN

ASDAN stands for Award Scheme Development and Accreditation Network, although the full title is rarely used. Its qualifications are approved by Ofqual (England), DCELLS (Wales), CCEA (Northern Ireland) and some are also approved by SCQF in Scotland.

The qualifications are designed to be taken by students who need accreditation which is mainly below the level of GCSE. Courses available include the Certificate of Personal Effectiveness (CoPE) and others which focus on Basic Skills, Key Skills and Life Skills.

St Piers School is a non-maintained school for over 70 pupils aged 5–19, although most of the pupils are of secondary age. The children's home was established about seven years ago, when an increasing number of children were appearing who needed a 52-week placement. The school could only offer 38 weeks a year and it was noticeable that pupils were not always able to receive the same level of stimulation away from school and were losing their skills over the holiday periods. The cost of places at the school depends on the severity of a child's needs. The school caters for children and young people with epilepsy and other neurological conditions, whose learning difficulties range from moderate (MLD) to profound and multiple learning difficulties (PMLD).

 Case study: St Piers School and Children's Centre

The school

St Piers is able to admit pupils from the age of five, but the majority are over eleven. The complexity of the pupils has increased in recent years. There is a sliding scale of fees, which are paid by the 40 or so local authorities that use the school. A few years ago, about half the pupils were in the higher price bracket; today, it is the great majority – 80% of the pupils have epilepsy and a range of other conditions as well, such as autism, ADHD, Tourette's etc., while 20% are accepted although they do not have epilepsy, but their neurological conditions mean that they benefit from a similar curriculum.

The ability range in the school used to be mostly MLD, but now around a third of the pupils fall in the SLD to PMLD range. The pupils are there as termly boarders. There are strong links between the school and the boarding houses, as many student support staff work in both environments.

The children's centre

The head teacher of the school has always been keen on the school being seen as part of the local community. Events, activities and celebrations are shared with local schools. When the local authority wanted to create a children's centre in the locality, the NCYPE was happy to provide a building and to be responsible for running it. After some initial apprehension on the part of families who wondered whether it was for children with medical needs, the children's centre has become well established as one of the Phase 2 children's centres offering:

- an information, support and advice drop-in service
- stay and play sessions for families and the under-5s
- a child health clinic
- parenting courses
- access to a breastfeeding counsellor
- a kickers and crawlers club
- a group for new parents
- an expectant parents group
- a dads and kids club
- a toy library.

Figure 6.9 (in Chapter 6) gives a chart showing a timeline for the development of the centre and lists the range of partnerships and other links that have been created in establishing it.

The National Centre for Young People with Epilepsy is running a national campaign to improve the lives of children and young people in the UK with epilepsy. The *Better Futures Campaign* will build on the NCYPE's wealth of knowledge and expertise to promote better services and understanding for young people with epilepsy.

The head teacher, Nick Byford, says:

> We offer our own form of inclusiveness, as pupils here are included in all that goes on. Sometimes, we have to persuade people in the local community that it is important for our pupils to be able to participate and use local facilities, such as the shops and the swimming pool.

Questions for reflection

- If children's centres are attached to schools, do you think it makes a difference whether they are attached to nursery, primary, secondary or special schools?
- What are the particular issues for special schools and their pupils in implementing the extended schools programme?
- What do you see as the overlap between what is offered by a children's centre and an extended school? Would it help to bring the programmes closer together in some way?

The next two case studies show the involvement of LAs in partnership working. The first is a description of an LA service for pupils with SEND that was quick off the mark in trying to make a reality of joined-up working between the services. The second is of a charity working with a local authority to bring a wide range of services together.

Integrated Disability Service, Warwickshire

One local authority SEN and disability service that was quick to adapt to a multi-agency approach is Warwickshire's Integrated Disability Service (IDS). Before the separate services began to merge, initial concerns about retaining separate identities were overcome by having a shadow management team in place. By 2006, a single line management structure was established. The team says that what really started to make a difference in bringing the teams together was the move, in 2007/08, to co-locate them. To start with, there were separate administrative teams for social care, health, and teaching and learning. Today, the teams have been fully integrated under a single line management structure and there is one route for all referrals.

The aspect of the service that is responsible for teaching and learning covers:

- family support for birth to three years
- pre-school
- SEN childcare
- autism

- hearing loss
- visual impairment
- physical disability
- children with severe and complex needs
- specific language disorders.

Led by the Service Development Managers, Jane Carter and Dilys Davies, who are line managed by someone from a social care background, their team includes teachers, teaching assistants, child development advisers, childcare co-ordinators and midday supervisors. The team's role is to provide additional expertise and support to complement the work of early years settings, primary, secondary and special schools.

Due to its established multi-agency approach, Warwickshire was selected to become one of the 16 speech, language and communication needs (SLCN) pathfinders. These were established as a result of the Bercow Review (DCSF and DoH, 2008b). The pilots run from September 2009 to September 2011.

 Key points: The Bercow Review

Shortly before becoming speaker of the House of Commons, John Bercow MP was asked by the DCSF and the Department of Health to review provision for SLCN. After an interim report, he produced: *The Bercow Report: A Review of Services for Children and Young People (0–19) with Speech, Language and Communication Needs* (DCSF and DoH, 2008b).

In December 2008, the Government published its response, *Better Communication: An Action Plan to Improve Services for Children and Young People with Speech, Language and Communication Needs* (DCSF, 2008e), which accepted most of Bercow's recommendations, including developing a commissioning framework through pathfinder pilots.

 Case study: Integrated Disability Service (IDS), Warwickshire

When it was appointed as one of the SLCN commissioning pathfinders, the IDS team was able to build on some of the work it had already been doing with schools, which included developing a training package to help schools create 'Communication Friendly Environments'. This has three strands:

- Strand 1: Survey of visual support systems currently in place
- Strand 2: Survey of communication – teachers adapt their presentation according to the environment and the situation
- Strand 3: Survey of the environment.

Through the experience of working with a number of schools, the team has built on this approach to fit in with the requirements of being part of a commissioning pathfinder.

(Continued)

(Continued)

A further factor that put the team in a strong position was the relationship that had been established over several years with Widget Software. This had resulted in the Symbols Inclusion Project, which was a collaboration between Widget Software and IDS. Since this started several years ago, the team has seconded a teacher and a teaching assistant to work part-time with the staff at Widget Software. This has led to a series of booklets being developed to support different areas of the curriculum. Each one has five versions, differentiated according to the level of understanding and the vocabulary of the user. Children have been involved in choosing the symbols they prefer for some of the signs. As the local authority has taken out a countywide licence, all the material, once developed, can be used across educational establishments and provides an ever-expanding range of resources, which have developed as a result of the partnership between Widget and IDS.

These resources are part of the training for schools, with all the schools involved using the same symbols. Although the materials were first developed for younger pupils, there are now materials for supporting subject-specific vocabulary at secondary level as well. This is proving useful in extending the work of IDS in the area of SLCN into the secondary phase, as well as increasing the scope of the pathfinder pilot. Developing communication-friendly environments also supports those who have learning difficulties, in addition to those who have speech, language and communication needs.

Warwickshire's Integrated Disability Service is an example of the benefits of joined-up working within a local authority.

The final case study is of a partnership between a charity established some years ago by parents and a local authority.

Partnership working between a charity and an LA – Nottingham Regional Society for Adults and Children with Autism (NORSACA)

In the past, the opportunity has not always been taken for charities responsible for educational settings and LAs to work closely together, with the result that expertise and enthusiasm is not shared as widely as it might be. This may be because an LA is busy looking after its own schools and linking with independent or non-maintained schools has not been seen as a priority, or because the charity involved has not thought it necessary to build up a relationship with the authority where it is situated, as its contacts are much wider than this. Many non-maintained and independent schools attract pupils from far beyond the area where they are located, particularly if they offer boarding accommodation. It is only in recent years that closer links have been encouraged between the independent, non-maintained and state sectors.

Today there is a great deal of talk about making it easier for parents to set up their own schools. In the 1960s, this was not such a usual concept.

This was when a group of parents living in Nottinghamshire were keen to establish educational provision for their children who were on the autism spectrum. They set up NORSACA, a charity which has grown to become a significant organisation. It established Sutherland House which is now a non-maintained special school catering for over 90 day pupils aged 3–19 who are on the autism spectrum. It has expanded over the years to occupy five sites in and around Nottingham. In 2008, Sutherland House was one of the first non-maintained schools to be awarded specialist status in communication and interaction. Being a specialist school has increased the links the school had already established with maintained schools in the area through its outreach service. Having these links makes it easier for pupils to gain some mainstream experience, if this forms part of their Individual Education Plan (IEP), or, in a few cases, to move across to a local school altogether.

One of the significant developments that has grown out of the original aim of establishing a school, has been a long-standing partnership between NORSACA and Nottinghamshire Local Authority. This provides an example of how, by joining forces, an organisation can offer a much more comprehensive service than either a charity or LA may be able to provide on its own. Through partnership working, NORSACA and Nottinghamshire LA have been able to share resources, accommodation, training and staffing, to provide a comprehensive package of education and support throughout the lives of those on the autism spectrum and their families. One of NORSACA's strategic objectives is: *To develop quality services through strategic partnership working*. This is not just something that is written on paper, but it has become an established way of working over many years and the service, working in tandem with Nottinghamshire LA for part of its provision, has continued to grow.

 Case study: Nottingham Regional Society for Adults and Children with Autism (NORSACA) and Nottinghamshire Local Authority

Through building up a close working partnership, NORSACA and Nottinghamshire LA are able to provide a range of services that would not have been achieved by either partner working on its own. These are based around four elements:

Family services:

- play schemes for children on the autism spectrum and their siblings
- sporting activities in conjunction with Nottinghamshire County's 'Football in the Community' scheme
- a Dads' Forum, which has regular meetings and a website, so that information and ideas can be shared.

(Continued)

(Continued)

Children's services:

- *the Early Communication and Autism Partnership (ECAP)* has been running since 2001 and supports young children under the age of four, their families and the early years settings in which they are placed.
- *the Elizabeth Newson Centre for Diagnosis and Assessment* assesses both children who may be admitted to Sutherland House School, and those who are referred by PCTs or LAs from anywhere in the UK. The centre specialises in the assessment of children who have disorders of development and communication.

Central services:

These are based in NORSACA's main building, Park Hall Autism Resource Centre, and provide the administrative support for all the charity's activities. Park Hall accommodates some of the training and other activities and events that are organised. A recent addition has been a Parents' Room, where parents and carers can socialise and share ideas and concerns.

Adult and Further Education services:

- a Further Education (FE) Unit run in conjunction with West Nottinghamshire College
- day service provision.

Parents are often concerned about points of transition, such as the move from one phase of education to another and from education to what happens when the child leaves school. This can be particularly problematic for those on the autism spectrum who are disturbed by change. These concerns have been minimised by NORSACA and Nottinghamshire LA working closely together to provide services from the early years right through to college and beyond. This breadth of provision illustrates clearly the value of pooling resources, experience and expertise.

Another benefit of the relationship that has been established between the charity and the LA has been the ability to attract funding for particular projects. For instance, a joint bid to the government resulted in the production of a video of effective practice, using examples of local mainstream schools. The LA arranged for every school in the authority to receive a copy. In this way, schools that have built up expertise in the field of autism and related disorders, have been able to influence and move forward the work of other schools.

This chapter has shown a number of different ways in which schools (state and non-maintained), services, charities and local authorities can provide more effectively for children and families with SEND through partnership working. Not only does this ensure that expertise and resources are shared, but it provides a better and more joined-up service, which is of particular benefit to the families of children who have SEND. Obviously, there is a great deal more work to be done to effect the massive changes that have been required of schools and services, but these examples help to show what can be achieved.

 Summary

This chapter has concentrated on the move for schools and services to work more closely together. The implementation of the extended schools programme, and, running alongside it, the development of children's centres, has been explained.

Examples were given of schools that run children's centres (one of which is also an extended school), a local authority support service that has become an integrated service, and a charity that has established a close working relationship with an LA to deliver services to people on the autism spectrum and their families throughout life.

Further reading

Anning, A. and Ball, M. (2008) *Improving Services for Young Children: From Sure Start to Children's Centre.* London: Sage.

Cheminais, R. (2007) *Extended Schools and Children's Centres: A Practical Guide.* Oxford: David Fulton/Routledge.

Department for Children, Schools and Families (2008) *The Bercow Report: A Review of Services for Children and Young People (0–19) with Speech, Language and Communication Needs.* Nottingham: DCSF Publications.

Department for Children, Schools and Families and the Department of Health (2008) *Better Communication: An Action Plan to Improve Services for Children and Young People with Speech, Language and Communication Needs.* Nottingham: DCSF publications. Available at www.teacher-net.gov.uk/publications.

Successful strategies for partnership working

This chapter has a different format, as it is built around some of the strategies used by schools to create effective partnerships. These are included as photocopiable pages, which can be used to provide ideas and to promote discussion. As the majority of strategies have already been referred to in previous chapters, descriptions are kept to a minimum. Although the first group of strategies relate to Chapter 1, which covered working in partnership with pupils and parents, the rest of the strategies are grouped under headings that go across the chapters.

Partnerships with pupils and parents

Chapter 1 considered the rise in recognising the importance of listening to the voice of the child and involving pupils in their learning, as well as listening to their views on how to improve the school from the pupils' point of view. One of the schools featured was Hounslow Town Primary School, which has used UNICEF's *Little Book of Children's Rights and Responsibilities* (2007) as a basis for teaching pupils about rights and responsibilities. Class rules created by the children follow this model and Figure 6.1. shows how this approach was used by the children to write a playground charter. (In the original version, photographs of pupils were used to illustrate the points, such as putting litter in the bin and lining up when the whistle blows).

Turning to the involvement of older students, Figure 6.2a shows how pupils' personal targets at The Hereford Academy (mentioned in Chapter 4), are written by them using the approach of the 5 Rs: *resourcefulness, resilience, readiness, reflectiveness and relationships*. The same format is used for both English and maths targets. This makes students think about their targets, not just in terms of subjects, but how they can apply the same approach across the different areas of learning. This also applies to supporting students with behavioural, emotional and social difficulties (BESD), where the Pupil Self-Assessment Questionnaire under these same headings is given as Figure 6.2b (see pages 90 and 91).

The Dacorum Education Support Centre, which was featured in Chapter 3, has a graduated approach to introducing students to the key stage 4 provision at the local college. Figure 6.3 shows the steps that are taken to involve them and their families from the time before the student starts, to continuing to keep them engaged throughout their time at the short stay school/PRU. This systematic approach has been found to be particularly valuable when trying to re-engage students who have failed to respond to other settings and has helped to prevent many from becoming NEETS (not in education, employment or training).

Hounslow Town Primary School Playground Charter

Our Rights	Our Responsibilities
It is our right to play and enjoy ourselves	It is our responsibility to be sensible and aware of others around us
It is our right to be safe something is	It is our responsibility to tell an adult when dangerous or we don't feel safe
It is our right to be treated kindly	It is our responsibility to respect everyone and listened to
It is our right to have a clean and tidy environment to play in	It is our responsibility to throw litter in the bin and put other things where they belong
It is our right to learn	It is our responsibility to stop on the first whistle, line up sensibly and walk into school ready to learn

Figure 6.1   Hounslow Town Primary School Playground Charter

 Photocopiable:

The Hereford Academy Pupil Personal Target

I will arrive on time for my lessons (resourcefulness/readiness) and make the most of my time down here by trying to achieve my personal best during the interventions (readiness/relationships/resilience/reflectiveness).

Resourcefulness:
My target is to …

Target achieved on …

Resilience:
My target is to …

Target achieved on …

Readiness:
My target is to …

Target achieved on …

Reflectiveness:
My target is to …

Target achieved on …

Relationships:
My target is to …

Target achieved on …

Figure 6.2a   The Hereford Academy Pupil Personal Target

Photocopiable:

The Hereford Academy Pupil Self-Assessment Questionnaire

This report is designed to help you know what you are good at, and where you would like to improve your performance.

- Read each statement and give yourself a performance standard between first and seventh (1st – a champion – you do this all the time. 7th – a poor performance/you do not currently do this).
- Choose one area from each section where you would like to do better at first, and circle it.

Resourcefulness (Respecting the Rules)

Res1	I arrive on time to my lessons	
Res2	I wear correct school uniform	
Res3	I am calm when entering and leaving the classroom	
Res4	I remain seated unless the teacher says I can move	
Res5	I sit properly on my chair	
Res6	I do what the teacher tells me to	
Res7	I stay in the classroom unless given permission to leave	
Res8	I put my hand up if I want to talk to the teacher	
Total score		

Standard	Silver	Gold	Olympic

(LSW circle as appropriate – if score is above 60 = Standard; between 50–60 = Silver; between 40–50 = Gold; less than 40 = Olympic)

Resilience (Self-respect)

Resi1	I don't give up, and ask for help	
Resi2	I tell people calmly if I feel upset, angry or hurt	
Resi3	I wait patiently for help	
Resi4	I like to be praised if I have done things well	
Resi5	I know when I have worked hard and done well	
Resi6	I know when I have done something wrong	
Resi7	I can look people in the eye	
Resi8	I say sorry and mean it if I have done something wrong	
Total score		

Standard	Silver	Gold	Olympic

(LSW circle as appropriate – if score is above 60 = Standard; between 50–60 = Silver; between 40–50 = Gold; less than 40 = Olympic)

(Continued)

Photocopiable:

(Continued)

Readiness

Red1	I bring all the correct equipment and books	
Red2	I will re-read and check work if I am asked	
Red3	I respect my own equipment and that of others	
Red4	I keep on target all lesson, and don't join in if others behave badly	
Red5	I can working independently without lots of reminders from the teacher	
Red6	I present my work tidily	
Red7	I settle to work quickly	
Red8	I complete my homework and hand it in on time	
Total score		

Standard	Silver	Gold	Olympic

(LSW circle as appropriate – if score is above 60 = Standard; between 50–60 = Silver; between 40–50 = Gold; less than 40 = Olympic)

Relationships

Rel1	I listen to the teacher when they are talking to me	
Rel2	I listen to an adult when they are talking to the whole class	
Rel3	I accept consequences from adults or friends	
Rel4	I use polite language, and don't swear	
Rel5	I respect other people's personal safety and am never physically aggressive	
Rel6	I don't talk too loudly or shout	
Rel7	I respect other people's right to a quiet working environment	
Rel8	I am sensitive to other people's feelings	
Total score		

Standard	Silver	Gold	Olympic

(LSW circle as appropriate – if score is above 60 = Standard; between 50–60 = Silver; between 40–50 = Gold; less than 40 = Olympic)

Reflectiveness

Ref1	I can wait my turn	
Ref2	I get on well with others when we work as a group	
Ref3	I make positive comments to others	
Ref4	I am liked by other pupils	
Ref5	I feel confident talking to adults	
Ref6	I tell the truth	
Ref7	I can stand up for myself in a way which does not get me told off	
Ref8	I can disagree with someone without having an argument	
Total score		

Standard	Silver	Gold	Olympic

(LSW circle as appropriate – if score is above 60 = Standard; between 50–60 = Silver; between 40–50 = Gold; less that 40 = Olympic)

Figure 6.2b   The Hereford Academy Pupil Self-Assessment Questionnaire

Photocopiable:

Dacorum Educational Support Centre Cr8 – Curriculum Development Model

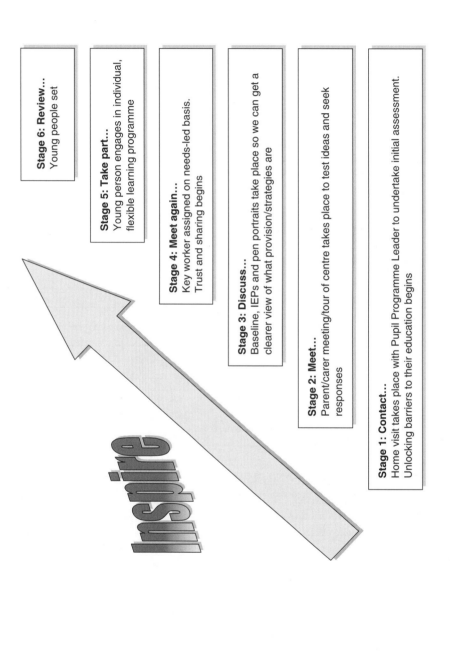

Stage 6: Review...
Young people set

Stage 5: Take part...
Young person engages in individual, flexible learning programme

Stage 4: Meet again...
Key worker assigned on needs-led basis. Trust and sharing begins

Stage 3: Discuss...
Baseline, IEPs and pen portraits take place so we can get a clearer view of what provision/strategies are

Stage 2: Meet...
Parent/carer meeting/tour of centre takes place to test ideas and seek responses

Stage 1: Contact...
Home visit takes place with Pupil Programme Leader to undertake initial assessment. Unlocking barriers to their education begins

Figure 6.3   Dacorum Educational Support Centre Cr8 – Curriculum Development Model – it's needs-led!

Photocopiable:

Partnership Working to Support Special Educational Needs and Disabilities © Rona Tutt, 2011, Sage Publications

Partnerships between staff, pupils and parents

Whereas the last example focused on the work done with individual families, the next example focuses on how modern technology has opened up new ways of staff, pupils and parents working together. The learning platform used at South Dartmoor (as described in Chapter 4) has made it possible for them all to have common access to some parts of the system, with other parts being restricted to particular groups. As pointed out previously, having information about what their children are learning and the progress they are making, has enabled parents to take a closer interest in their child's education, as well as being in a better position to offer them support. The assistant head teacher responsible for ICT has given his top tips for getting such a system off the ground. These are provided as Figure 6.4.

Another example of how all parties can work more closely together was provided in Chapter 3 by the Greys Education Centre. By using e-learning, the Centre has a partnership approach with schools, key stage 4 students and their families. Parents can be involved in supporting their young people and the students have some choice over where and when they learn. Figure 6.5 gives the Centre's guidelines for creating an effective e-learning provision. The information in the final box refers to Assessment for Learning (AFL) and visual, auditory and kinaesthetic (VAK) learning styles.

Staffing structures for partnership working

In order to take on the increasing demands placed on schools, many school leaders have embraced a model of *distributed leadership*, where responsibilities are shared across a team of staff, rather than head teachers or principals carrying much of the load. The St Marylebone School, a specialist school whose third specialism is in communication and interaction, was described in Chapter 2. As each new specialism has become part of the school's work, staff have adjusted their roles to take on new responsibilities. Figure 6.6 shows how the communication and interaction strand has been woven across the school's management structure, to ensure that this newer element is fully integrated into the work of the school. (PLTS in the centre box at the bottom of the page refers to Personal, Learning and Thinking Skills. This is part of the secondary curriculum and includes: team working, independent inquiry, self-management, reflective learning, effective participation and creative thinking).

South Dartmoor Community College – top tips for harnessing parent power

- Roll out in order of audience number (i.e. to teachers, to students, to parents)

- Do not under-estimate the vast range of parents. They are the widest mixed-ability group

- Incorporate enough admin support into planning

- Consider roll-out in terms of manageability – do you roll out in 'chunks', e.g. a year group at a time, or do you go for access to all?

- Stick to your planned roll-out – don't let others divert you from the main task at hand

- Test thoroughly before rolling out

- Involve your 'Pastoral Team' (assume here that Senior Leadership Team (SLT) involvement goes without saying!)

- Plan for parent training – use students … if you have followed advice in first top tip

- Include as many reasons for parents needing to use the learning gateway as possible – promote usage

- Cater for disbanding, or phasing out old-style communicating

- Give all audiences as much information as you can, as often as you can

- Review internal procedures if necessary, e.g. assessment procedures

- Be brave enough to plan to withhold parts until you are ready

- Have a considered plan about the 'hard to reach'

Figure 6.4   South Dartmoor Community College – top tips for harnessing parent power

 Photocopiable:

Greys Education Centre – What makes a sucessful e-learning provision

Student and parent interviews	Agreed personalised targets
Peer mentors	Laptop/mobile dongle for 24/7 access
Small groups with key worker	Full tech training for all
Robust ICT environment	AFL/VAK resources

Figure 6.5   Greys Education Centre – What makes a successful e-learning provision

Photocopiable:

Partnership Working to Support Special Educational Needs and Disabilities © Rona Tutt, 2011, Sage Publications

The St Marylebone School SEN Specialism – Communication and Interaction Team 2009/2010

The Communication and Interaction team is woven horizontally across the whole school management structure. There are departments that feed into the team that are also managed under the pupil achievement and personalising learning arms of the school.

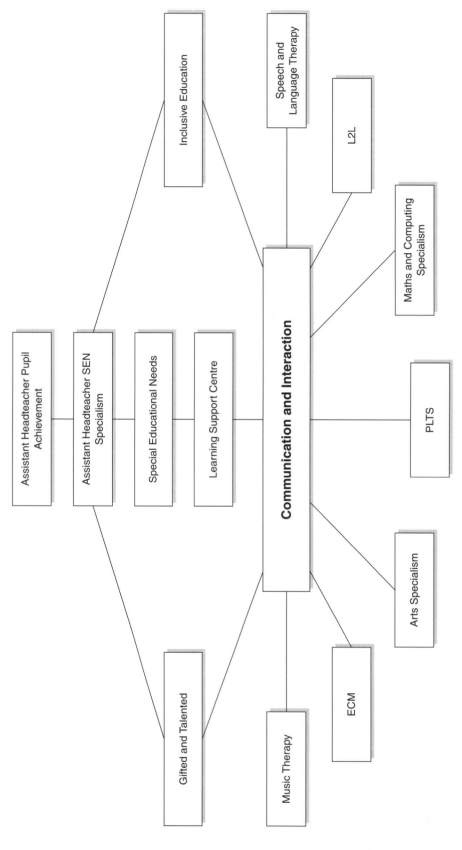

Figure 6.6   The St Marylebone School SEN Specialism – Communication and Interaction Team 2009/10

Photocopiable:

Partnership Working to Support Special Educational Needs and Disabilities © Rona Tutt, 2011, Sage Publications

Sharing resources

As a result of becoming a specialist school with a specialism in cognition and learning, Barrs Court (which was described in Chapter 2) has used its specialism to develop curriculum models for children who, regardless of their chronological age, are at a very early stage of thinking. These are used with some of the pupils in the school and also made available to other schools. Figure 6.7 shows how the approach to pupils with very significant needs has been tackled for Early Thinking Skills. The contents page is given, showing what is covered in the different sections of this resource.

Woodlands High School was described in Chapter 4 for its work on designing a new course for students who are not able to cope with GCSE. This was developed in conjunction with local businesses, to ensure that students would develop the requisite skills to access work experience opportunities and enhance their chances of employment. A business link with Primus Training enabled the school to market its Vocational Awards to other schools in Wales and England. The five courses in Moving On Up and the business links that helped to create it are shown as Figure 6.8.

A panoply of partnerships

To end this chapter, a couple of mind maps are given which demonstrate the extent to which partnership working has become a way of life for children's centres and for schools. When St Piers first started setting up its children's centre in conjunction with the local authority (as described in the previous chapter), it had to carve out a whole range of partnerships and outside links. These are shown in Figure 6.9., which also gives a timeline for the development of the children's centre. Similarly, Furze Down, a special school in Buckinghamshire (which has not been mentioned previously), has mapped out the multiplicity of links that form part of its work with children who have complex needs. The school is also a specialist school in communication and interaction. Starting from putting the child and his or her needs at the centre, Figure 6.10. shows the complexity of the interrelationship between a school and the agencies that help to support children and families.

Barrs Court School – The Specialist Curriculum for Early Thinking Skills

Section	Contents
One	Introduction • Specialist curricula for pupils with PMLD • Context to sensory and perceptual impairment in pupils with PMLD • Context to cognitive impairment in pupils with PMLD • Maths and Science for pupils with PMLD • Using the curriculum for Early Thinking Skills
Two	Strategies • Tools for learning • Creating responsive environments • Developing body awareness and self-image • Making choices • Using multi-sensory environments • Using switches and access devices • Using resonance boards and Soundbeam • Developing fundamental maths skills • Developing problem-solving skills • Recognising and understanding patterns • Developing object permanence • Experiencing simple counting and number
Three	The Early Thinking Skills Curriculum • Visual development • Auditory development • Tactile development • Cognitive development
Four	Maths and Science at P Levels 1–4 • QCA guidance on the development of thinking skills • NC Maths for pupils with PMLD • NC Science for pupils with PMLD • Implementing the National Numeracy Strategy • Recognising attainment: levels of experience • Specialist curriculum links to National Curriculum • Maths and Science at P Levels 1–4 including performance indicators, teaching activities and suggested resources
Five	Appendices • Explanation of coding • Suggested equipment and resources for the development of Early Thinking Skills • List of equipment suppliers • Useful journals/periodicals • References and suggested further reading

Figure 6.7   Barrs Court School – The Specialist Curriculum for Early Thinking Skills

 Photocopiable:

Partnership Working to Support Special Educational Needs and Disabilities © Rona Tutt, 2011, Sage Publications

Woodlands High School – Moving On Up Vocational Awards

Already established links through work experience

```
                                            Moving On Up
                                            Garden and Park
                                            Skills Award
                                                                    Moving On Up
                                                                    Basic Work Skills
                                                                    Award

                        Cardiff Council                       mentioned need for
                        Parks Department                      understanding of work

                                                         Cardiff Council
                                                         Catering Department
      LP met                                  LP met
      with                                    with
                        Moving On Up                               Moving On Up
                        Vocational                                 Basic Cafe and Restaurant
                        Awards                                     Skills Award

   'Sponsor a                                 LP met
   School'                 joint idea         with
   Programme                                              Moving On Up
                                                          Office Skills Award
      Cardiff Devils                          Welsh Assembly
      Ice Hockey Team        Primus           Government

                          adopted by

   regular visits                             Moving On Up
   and support of                             Intro to IT Award
   school                   Work experience
      Woodlands             opportunities
                                                          already established links
                                                          through work experience

                                                          work experience opportunities
```

Figure 6.8   Woodlands High School – Moving On Up Vocational Awards

Photocopiable:

Partnership Working to Support Special Educational Needs and Disabilities © Rona Tutt, 2011, Sage Publications

St Piers' range of services

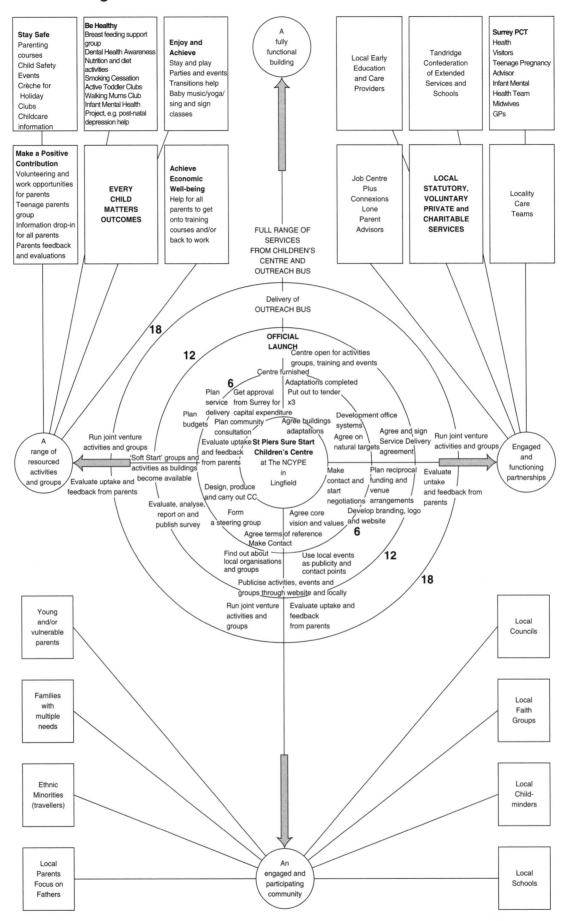

Figure 6.9   St Piers' range of services

Furze Down School – pupil access and support spider diagram

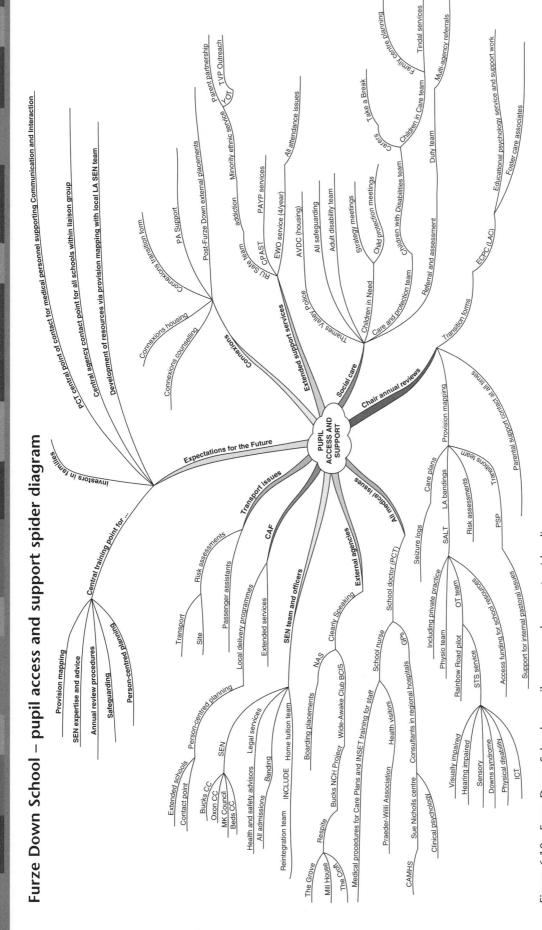

Figure 6.10   Furze Down School – pupil access and support spider diagram.
*Created by, Heather Wyatt

The strategies in this chapter show different ways in which partnership working is coming to the fore, to the extent that it is now a crucial part of the way schools and services operate. Personalising learning, meeting the five outcomes of Every Child Matters and supporting children and young people with a wide range of needs, mean that it is essential for everyone involved to pool their expertise, their ideas and their resources. The concluding chapter will examine how partnership working is likely to develop in the light of the diversification of schools and the need to individualise learning to meet the needs of all children and young people.

Conclusion

This book has looked at the changing nature of schools and services and the effect this has had on children and young people who have special educational needs and disabilities (SEND). These changes have led to educational settings forming or strengthening a number of different kinds of partnerships. Reference has also been made to the fact that schools of all types are experiencing a more complex population of pupils, which makes it even more necessary for experience and expertise to be shared. In drawing the threads of this book together, the following questions will be addressed:

- What contributes to the success of partnership working?
- How did schools and other settings use a change in their structure or status to support children and young people with SEND?
- Was it as a result of changes in the way they were working that enabled them to improve opportunities for these pupils?
- How might future developments assist in the education of children and young people with SEND?

The ingredients for successful partnerships

The elements that make for successful partnership working in the context of schools and services can be summarised in terms of: the attitudes and attributes of school leaders; the outlook and flexibility of the staff team; and how any changes from one situation to another are managed.

School leaders and distributed leadership

Although the case studies were chosen to illustrate a wide range of schools and services, it was interesting to note that those who were leading them had much in common. Firstly, they had a very clear idea of how they wanted their organisations to develop. Secondly, they interpreted new challenges as opportunities that could help them to realise their vision. Thirdly, they were not afraid to take risks and to try something different, whether it was creating new partnerships, harnessing new technology, or creating new leadership and management structures.

As the pressures on schools to raise standards and to take on new responsibilities have increased, the idea of a having a single person at the helm to mastermind everything, has given way to the idea of distributed leadership, where roles and responsibilities are divided between

103

staff in positions of seniority. An example of this was given in the previous chapter (Figure 6.6), which showed how The St Marylebone School's specialism in communication and interaction has been absorbed by integrating the responsibilities into the work of the school management structure. At Darlington Education Village (see Chapter 3), after trying separate leadership teams for each school under one executive head teacher, there is now a single leadership team taking responsibility for different areas of teaching and learning across the three schools. Distributed leadership works well when the key players are prepared to be flexible in order to meet changing circumstances, rather than being territorial about their roles. Along with being a leader who is prepared to share responsibilities and to seize opportunities, he or she needs to create an atmosphere where the whole staff team is prepared to work together, even when this means embracing change.

The leadership of change

Much has been written by other authors about the need to manage change, which can often be an uncomfortable process, even when the outcome is generally agreed to be desirable. Not everyone finds it easy to take on board new ideas and new ways of working. At the present time, there has been such a surfeit of change that there can be an understandable resistance to trying out fresh ideas. There have been several references in the book to the need not to rush change, but to allow time for each stage to become embedded before taking the next step. The leaders of the Integrated Disability Service (as mentioned in Chapter 5) showed the steps that had been taken in order to make a radical change acceptable to the staff working in previously separate services. This was achieved by:

1. Deciding on a new structure
2. Putting a shadow leadership team in place
3. Co-locating teams from across education, social care and health, but retaining separate administrative teams
4. Amalgamating the administrative support.

The leadership of change involves leaders knowing where they are taking their organisation and being able to convey that vision to others. It means seeking to make sure that all those concerned feel involved in the process and that there is clarity about how roles and responsibilities may need to be adjusted.

Staff teams

As more is expected of schools and as they work alongside other services, sponsors, partners and organisations, those already in post are taking on new responsibilities and additional posts are also being created. Barrs Court, whose case study appeared in Chapter 2, has established a major role for teaching assistants who have become Instructors in Disability, to ensure that all staff are aware, and keep in mind, the communication, physical and sensory needs of the pupils. The list of some of the staff who make up the team at Goddard Park (an integrated extended primary school and children's centre described in Chapter 5) includes family support workers, childcare development workers, a community learning mentor and playleaders. Not only are teaching staff and support staff developing new roles, but they are learning to work alongside colleagues from other backgrounds. The key to the success of these extended teams of staff working in schools and services is their ability to be flexible in terms of adjusting their own roles and in welcoming a wider range of expertise.

Types of partnerships and pupils with SEND

Chapter 1 began by looking at how partnerships with pupils and parents have changed significantly over the years and at how these partnerships continue to evolve. Not only must the staff work as a team in the development of a school or service, but pupils and their families need to be involved in the process of school improvement, too.

Partnerships with pupils

Undoubtedly, schools have come a long way in finding ways of engaging pupils. The 'chalk and talk' days of the past, where teachers did most of the talking and pupils were seen as being there to absorb information, have long passed. Chapter 1 gave examples of how children are being consulted and involved, including those like the children at Grangewood School who have limited cognitive ability, or those at St Vincent's school who are blind or visually impaired. The pupils at Shiremoor Primary School learn how to run committees by having a school council called the Stay Safe and Happy Management Committee, while those at Hounslow Town Primary School, where the UNICEF *Children's Rights and Responsibilities* (2007) booklet is displayed in every classroom, are familiar with using this approach to create their own charters (see Figure 6.1 in Chapter 6). Whatever the age of the child or the nature of any learning difficulties, involving them in their learning and inviting their ideas on how to improve the school as a whole, helps them to feel engaged and even excited by the process of education.

Personalising learning
The drive to personalise learning, which has been a feature of the way schools include pupils in their learning for many years, is part of the move to make students feel that staff are working in partnership with them. In

Leadbetter's (2008) book, *What's Next? 21 Ideas for 21st Century Learning*, he talks of learning being most effective when it is personalised. He points out that in order to do this, people need to feel involved in their learning, and that, in turn, means sustained and consistent relationships:

Relationships   →   Participation   →   Personalised learning

It was mentioned earlier that there was some natural resistance to this approach when it was first introduced, because it was feared that it would be impracticable. However, Leadbetter suggests it can be achieved by being more flexible about when and where learning takes place, varying the pace at which students are expected to learn, allowing them to learn in different ways, and teaching them the skills that will help them become better learners.

This last point is reminiscent of The Hereford Academy's approach of teaching students (and staff) to develop the skills of Resourcefulness, Resilience, Readiness, Reflectiveness and Relationships. (Examples of this approach were given in Chapter 6 Figures 6.2a and 6.2b).

Partnerships with families

This is an era when people expect to have a greater degree of choice in all aspects of their lives and to be consulted about what happens to them. In the context of school, this means recognising the importance, not just of pupil voice, but the involvement of parents and carers as well. In any case, as has been mentioned previously, it is somewhat arbitrary to talk about children separately from their families. Parents are seen, quite rightly, as their children's first educators and, once a child is in school, it makes no sense for their families to feel detached from the learning process. Dealing with students who have failed previously to respond to a more traditional learning environment, Dacorum Education Support Centre (as described in Chapter 3) has a carefully staged approach to involving students and families from the start. (This appeared in Chapter 6, Figure 6.3.) The imaginative use of new technologies is making it easier for staff, pupils and families to share information and to gain a greater sense of working together. This was demonstrated by South Dartmoor Community College's use of a learning gateway (see Chapter 6, Figure 6.4) and the e-learning approach of Greys Education Centre (see Chapter 6, Figure 6.5).

Sometimes, the push to be involved has come from parents rather than from schools, as was seen through the work of NORSACA, where the parents' fight for provision was described in Chapter 5. Making it easier for parents to open their own schools is something that is very much to the fore at the moment.

Once the relationships within a school are working and between staff, pupils and families, there is the array of partnerships schools are forming with other schools and with the wider community of the world of business, and, crucially for those with SEND, with other services: health and social care. Vulnerable pupils and families are more likely to need the support of health and social care as well as education.

Partnerships between schools

In his final report, *Learning Behaviour: Lessons Learned* (DCSF, 2009a), Steer mentioned the key characteristics of successful partnerships, in terms of the behaviour and attendance partnerships between schools. This is one of the partnerships for a specific purpose that secondary schools must now have. Although Steer was referring, in particular, to this type of partnership, some of his points have a wider application:

- the active engagement of all members of the partnership
- the inclusion of Pupil Referral Units (PRUs) and any other major providers of alternative provision
- the engagement of primary schools and FE colleges
- the alignment of behaviour and attendance partnership with the local Safer School Partnership
- the engagement with extended services
- clear protocols for pupil managed moves and for the placement of 'hard to place' pupils
- a focus on early intervention.

The first point is key to the success of any type of partnership working and the examples given in this book have been of partnerships that were successful because of the involvement of all concerned. There may have been adjustments to be made along the way, for it is never as easy to change attitudes as it is to change structures, but, ultimately, the changes worked because people collaborated to make them happen. The kinds of developments there are today, such as 14–19 consortia and extended school clusters, mean that collaboration between schools has become a vital part of their role, quite apart from the collaborative working that has developed through schools taking on a new identity.

Specialist schools

The dramatic increase in the number of specialist schools, with a curriculum, a SEN specialism, or both, has been a significant way of spreading expertise between schools. Both Corbets Tey and Shaftesbury High School (as illustrated in their case studies in Chapter 2) have used their specialist status to create centres for training and developing staff, while other examples showed how materials were being developed to support people's understanding of pupils with SEND. The Specialist Schools Programme has also brought in the non-maintained sector, which has expertise in helping pupils with complex needs. There seems little doubt that, in the same way that knowledge of curriculum areas has been strengthened by having specialist schools, the same could be said of the value of having an increasing number of schools with a SEN specialism. This development would be enhanced further by allowing independent special schools to participate in the programme and by encouraging more mainstream schools to become involved. The latter is unlikely to happen while schools are judged largely on the academic achievements of their students.

Co-located and federated schools

Chapter 3 looked at co-located and federated schools, which is another way in which expertise, facilities and staffing can more easily be shared across mainstream and special schools and across primary and secondary schools. The examples from Guernsey showed the benefits of co-location, where the secondary special school has been co-located with a mainstream secondary school, while the primary special school has been co-located with other services, making it much easier for parents of pupils with SEND to access the support they need. Such close working also makes it easier for children to transfer between settings, or to have wider opportunities for mixing and learning with a broader peer group. The model of co-location plus federation exemplified by the Darlington Education Village, which operates as three schools under one roof and one leadership team, raises the question of how far the divide between primary and secondary and between special and mainstream schools is likely to persist in the future. Whether or not it does so, it is clear that working more closely together is benefiting all concerned.

Academies, trust schools and other business links

Academies and trust schools draw on a broader range of knowledge and experience through working with sponsors and partners, both from within and beyond educational circles. In Chapter 4, the case studies explored some very different establishments, yet all could show that the involvement of a broader range of organisations is bringing in additional perspectives and wider opportunities. The Hereford Academy's range of sponsors and partners has given students direct links to higher education as well as to the world of work, opening up opportunities for students of all abilities, while the partnerships connected with South Dartmoor Community College's trust status has linked it with a university's educational research department, including researching into improving outcomes for pupils with SEND, as well as an organisation that helps to train parents in the use of technology in the home. The St Christopher School has used its Trust status to enhance people's understanding of children and young people who have autism and ADHD. Although schools in Wales do not have the option of becoming academies or trust schools, many have very strong links with businesses. This was illustrated by Woodlands School, where the network of business links leading to the creation of a new award called Moving On Up, was illustrated in Figure 6.8.

Extended schools and children's centres

One of the ways in which the joining up of services is forging ahead is through the extended schools and children's centres' agenda. Schools are becoming extended schools in three senses of the word:

1. extending the hours the school is open
2. extending the range of activities provided, often in collaboration with the private, voluntary and independent sector (PVI)
3. extending the number of services the school hosts, or signposts to where they are available.

As every school becomes an extended school, and more children's centres are attached to primary, secondary and special schools, it becomes easier to have joined-up working with families as well as the wider community. The example of Goddard Park, which is run as an integrated primary school and children's centre, shows what can be achieved, both in terms of earlier identification of children with SEND and the move to meaningful parental involvement. The school opens its doors to learners of all ages and some parents have taken the opportunity to learn alongside their children and are provided with tutors in order to do so. St Piers School is an example of a non-maintained school linking with a local authority to provide a children's centre and in Chapter 6 (Figure 6.9) there was an illustration of the wealth of links that this new way of working has created. It is the children and young people with SEND and their families who benefit the most from the ready access to services that children's centres and extended schools can provide.

Although some of these developments could have been achieved without the schools taking on the particular structure or role they acquired, there is no doubt that, in the examples given, the impetus given by a change in status, whether through feeling freer to innovate, having extra resources or developing new partnerships, has had a positive effect on children and young people with SEND, by opening up greater reserves of expertise and a wider range of opportunities. This book was never going to be about comparing one type of provision with another, but rather of drawing out from each how the change in the school's structure or status has led to improvements for its own pupils and those in the schools with which it has formed partnerships. In addition, it has to be remembered that schools are becoming ever more diverse and complex, so that they do not fall into only one category. All schools are expected to be part of the extended schools programme, most secondary schools and a growing number of special schools are specialist schools, but schools may also be co-located, federated or become trust schools, which makes it even less possible to compare one type of school with another. So what does all this tell us about how children with SEND may be supported in the future?

Future developments

At a time when change is accelerating and is unlikely to slow down, when the financial climate is uncertain and the political complexion of the country has altered, it is not easy to say what will happen in educational terms to children and young people who have special educational needs and disabilities. However, certain elements seem fairly clear.

Firstly, schools and services are likely to continue to evolve and diversify. The Academies Act will increase the number of schools that can be given this status (see Chapter 4), as well as enabling parents, teachers and other interested parties to establish 'Free Schools' from September 2011. Hopefully, this will mean that schools will continue to seek to find more holistic ways of meeting the needs of those who have learning difficulties or who find learning difficult because other factors get in the way of their ability to learn.

However, there are concerns that the further fragmentation of LAs could put at risk the provision and support for pupils with SEND. There is a long way to go in joining up the services, but, where it is beginning to work, it is the children and families who need the services the most that gain the most benefit. Children's centres are helping to offer support to the pre-school child and to identify any difficulties early on. Extended schools are providing activities and opportunities for learning and for enjoyment beyond the school day, which can mean additional stimulation for those with delayed development.

Secondly, the burgeoning number of partnerships that have been highlighted in this book, will continue to grow. Now that the world of schooling has been opened up, it will not go back to that secret garden from which it started to escape many decades ago. Pupils and their parents will expect to be recognised as true partners in the process, schools and services will continue to move towards collaborating across previous divides, whether mainstream and special, primary and secondary, independent and state, or across the services that are so essential to pupils' well-being of education, health and social care.

Thirdly, the personalising of learning is likely to continue, partly because it is becoming easier to deliver it through the flexibility of where and when learning takes place, including 24-hour access to the internet, and partly because older students are becoming used to moving between different schools, college and the workplace. Whether or not this will reach a point when the need to describe some children as having SEND disappears is not clear, but if that happens, it should not mean that a continuum of provision from in-class support at one end to 52-week placements at the other extreme will not be necessary, but simply that every child's individual interests, aptitudes and abilities will be recognised and provided for.

It was stated near the start of the book that not only have schools become more complex places, but children's needs are becoming more complex as well. To the list of reviews, reports and inquiries that have been mentioned previously, two more should be added. The Salt Review, which was published in March 2010, has made recommendations that will help to create a workforce able to meet the needs of the growing number of children who have profound and multiple learning difficulties (PMLD). From 2009 to 2011, the government is funding a Complex Learning Difficulties and Disabilities (CLDD) Research Project, to look at how best to meet the needs of children and young people who have co-existing conditions, such as autism and ADHD; children with recently discovered syndromes (although each one may be rare in itself, an increasing number are being identified); and those whose difficulties arise from being born at an age when they would not previously have survived and whose brain development may be incomplete. It is by working in partnership across schools, across different services and by sharing knowledge derived from different disciplines, that it will be possible to meet the needs of all children and young people. By opening up the full range of opportunities from different providers, whether within or beyond traditional educational circles, and working in partnership with them, previous barriers should continue to be broken down and the lives of all children and young people, including those who have special educational needs and disabilities, should be enriched.

Glossary

Academies   state funded independent schools, as they are independent of local authorities (LAs)

Alternative provision   education outside mainstream or special schools

Behaviour and attendance partnerships   a requirement in secondary schools, through which they work collaboratively to support pupils whose behaviour or attendance is unsatisfactory

Behaviour, emotional and social development/difficulties (BESD)   one of the four strands of need set out in the SEN Code of Practice.

Building Learning Power   an approach developed by Guy Claxton to help children and young people learn how to learn

Building Schools for the Future (BSF)   a programme started in 2004 with the aim of renewing all 3500 secondary schools in England by 2020

Choice advisers   a role designed to support parents who need help in finding their way around the education system, particularly in relation to choosing schools

Cognition and learning   one of the four strands of need set out in the SEN Code of Practice

Co-located schools and services   schools and services which share a site and may or may not be physically attached

Communication and interaction   one of the four strands of need set out in the SEN Code of Practice

Consortium of all-through schooling (CATS)   works with schools and local authorities in developing plans for all-through schooling structures

Core Entitlement   in the context of pupils in alternative provision, refers to the minimum entitlement that must be provided as part of full-time education

Department for Children, Education, Lifelong Learning and Skills (DCELLS)   the equivalent in Wales to the DfE

Distributed leadership   a term used for sharing out roles and responsibilities between a team of senior staff

Every Child Matters (ECM)   the Green Paper that preceded the Children Act 2004 and contains the five objectives of being healthy, keeping safe, enjoying and achieving, making a positive contribution and achieving economic well-being

Extended schools   came about as a result of the Children Act 2004. By 2010, every school is expected to open for longer, offer a range of activities (in conjunction with other partners and services), including for families and the local community

Federated schools   may retain their own governing bodies but have joint committees with delegated powers (known as collaborative governance), or may share a governing body

Foetal alcohol syndrome disorder (FASD)   a condition caused by the mother consuming alcohol, resulting in abnormal brain development before birth

Forest schools   schools run by leaders who are trained to support children's learning outdoors, where they learn a range of skills through interacting with the natural environment

14–19 consortia   consortia set up to assist the roll-out of the diplomas, so that schools can work together on delivering this extensive programme

'Free schools'   introduced by the Coalition Government to enable parents, teachers, charities and voluntary bodies to establish schools.

Grant Maintained Schools   these were abolished by the School Standards and Framework Act of 1998

High Performing Specialist School (HPSS)   a status awarded to specialist schools that have achieved excellent results

Information Passports   documents which include the personal details, data about previous attainments and other agency involvement, as well as the interests and aspirations for the future of any pupil who is in alternative provision for five or more days

Intensive Interaction   a method developed in the 1980s as a way of teaching the fundamentals of pre-speech communication to people of all ages who are at a very early stage of developing their skills

Lamb Inquiry   an inquiry established by the government to look at ways of increasing parental confidence in the SEN system

Learning and Skills Council (LSC)   a council established in 2001 to plan and fund all post-16 provision except higher education. It was replaced in April 2010 by the Young People's Learning Agency (YPLA) and the Skills Funding Agency (SFA), with some of its duties reverting to LAs

Library Boards   the term used in Northern Ireland for local education authorities (LEAs)

Local Education Authority (LEA)   a term still used in Wales, but in England has been largely replaced by Local Authorities (LAs), as part of the move to join up services

Managed move   the term used when a group of schools agree between them that a pupil would benefit from a fresh start in another school

Midday Supervisory Assistants (MSAs)   the term which has replaced the old term *dinner ladies*

National Challenge   a programme launched in June 2008 with the aim of tackling underachievement in secondary schools and improving results

National Council for Educational Excellence (NCEE)   a council set up in 2007 to draw together representatives from business, higher and further education, schools and early years settings

Non-maintained schools   special schools where, although the schools are not part of the state system, the fees are paid by the local authority rather than by parents (as happens in Independent Schools)

Parent councils   a requirement in Trust Schools, if the majority of governors are appointed and not elected. Other schools can choose whether or not to have a parent council

Parent Partnership Services (PPS)   a statutory requirement for local authorities to provide support to parents and carers of children with SEND

Parent Support Advisers (PSAs)   a link between home and school to support families

Personal Learning Plans   plans for pupils who are in alternative provision for at least ten days. They identify their educational needs, set clear goals and targets and specify their intended destination

Personalised Learning and Thinking Skills   team working, independent inquiry, self-management, reflective learning, effective participation and creative thinking

Primary Capital Programme (PCP)   a programme which aims to renew half of all primary schools by 2022/23, including giving them space to offer a wider range of services for children, families and the community

Private Finance Initiative   a form of public–private partnership (PPP) that increases the involvement of the private sector in the provision of public services' capital assets without owning them

Pupil Referral Unit (PRU)   *see* Short stay school

Raising the participation age   legislation that means that young people must be in education, training or work-based learning. This applies to17-year-olds by 2013 and to 18-year-olds by 2015

Reading Recovery   a method originating from New Zealand that gives one-to-one support to young children in establishing literacy skills

Reggio Emilia   an approach to early years education that places an emphasis on children being able to interact with the natural environment as well as with people

Rights Respecting School Award (RRSA)   an award started by UNICEF UK in 2004 and now running in more than 1000 primary and secondary schools in England, Northern Ireland, Scotland and Wales

Sensory and/or physical needs   one of the four strands of need set out in the SEN Code of Practice

Short stay school   under the Apprenticeships, Skills, Children and Learning Act of 2009, Pupil Referral Units (PRUs) were renamed short stay schools from September 2010. They are a form of alternative provision for pupils who cannot be in ordinary schools, mainly due to being excluded

Skills Funding Agency (SFA)   an agency created as part of the replacement for the Learning and Skills Council (LSC), to distribute funding for post-19 learners

Specialist Schools and Academies Trust   previously known as the Specialist Schools Trust, it expanded its title when taking on the academies as well. It is also involved with trust schools

Tellus surveys   annual surveys in the form of an online questionnaire designed to collect children's views on their lives, their schools and their local area

Tourette's syndrome   known in full as Gilles de la Tourette's syndrome. It is thought to arise from a neurological impairment of the central nervous system and results in both vocal and motor tics

Trust schools   foundation schools which are supported by a charitable foundation or 'trust'

UN Convention on the Rights of the Child (UNCRC)   a United Nations charter, that gives children throughout the world certain rights. It has been signed by most countries and has been in force in England since 1992

University Technical Colleges a scheme supported by Lord Baker to offer a more hands-on education to 14–19 year olds. First two due to open September 2010.

Virtual learning environments (VLEs)   a use of computers to enable the user to have access to remote learning, including a range of learning resources

Young People's Learning Agency (YPLA)   an agency created to take over some of the Learning and Skills Council's duties by supporting LAs in providing for learners aged 16–19, or for those with learning difficulties and disabilities (LLDD), up to the age of 25

Useful addresses

Consortium of All-Through Schooling (CATS)
The Glebe
Ipsley Lane
Redditch
B98 OAP
Tel: 01527 529461

Mencap
123 Golden Lane
London
EC1Y ORT
email: information@mencap.org.uk
Tel: 020 7454 0454

National Association of Independent and Non-Maintained Special Schools (NASS)
PO Box 705
York
YO30 6WW
Tel/fax: 01904 624446

National Association of Special Educational Needs (nasen)
nasen House
4/5 Amber Business Village
Amber Close
Amington
Tamworth
B77 4RP
email: welcome@nasen.org.uk
Tel: 01827 311500

Specialist Schools and Academies Trust (SSAT)
16th Floor
Millbank Tower

21–24 Millbank
London
SW1P 4QP
email: info@ssatrust.org.uk
Tel: 020 7802 2345

UNICEF's website – www.unicef.org.uk

UNICEF's website for children and young people – www.therightssite.org.uk

References and further reading

Anning, A. and Ball, M. (2008) *Improving Services for Young Children: From Sure Start to Children's Centre.* London: Sage.

Cameron, C., Moss, P., Owen, C., Petrie, P., Potts, P., Simmon, A. and Wigfall, V. (2009) *Working Together in Extended Schools and Children's Centres: A Study of Inter-professional Activity in England and Sweden.* Available at dcsf.gov.uk/everychildmatters/research

Cheminais, R. (2007) *Extended Schools and Children's Centres: A Practical Guide.* Oxford: David Fulton/Routledge.

Claxton, G. (2002) *Building Learning Power: Helping Young People to Become Better Learners.* Bristol: TLO.

Department for Children, Schools and Families (2007a) *The Children's Plan: Building Brighter Futures.* Norwich: The Stationery Office.

Department for Children, Schools and Families (2007b) *Extended Schools: Building on Experience.* Nottingham: DCSF Publications.

Department for Children, Schools and Families (2008a) *Quality Standards for Special Educational Needs (SEN) and Support and Outreach Services.* Nottingham: DCSF Publications.

Department for Children, Schools and Families (2008b) *Personalised Learning – A Practical Guide.* Available at www.publications.teachernet.gov.uk

Department for Children, Schools and Families (2008c) *The Children's Plan One Year On: A Progress Report.* Available at www.teachernet.gov.uk/publications

Department for Children, Schools and Families (2008d) *Special Educational Needs (SEN) Information Act.* Norwich: The Stationery Office.

Department for Children, Schools and Families (2008e) *Better Communication: An Action Plan to Improve Services for Children and Young People with Speech, Language and Communication Needs.* Nottingham: DCSF Publications.

Department for Children, Schools and Families (2008f) *Back on Track – A Strategy for Modernising Alternative Provision for Young People.* Available at www.teachernet.gov.uk/publications

Department for Children, Schools and Families (2008g) *Taking Back on Track Forward.* Available at www.teachernet.gov.uk/publications

Department for Children, Schools and Families (2008h) *Building Stronger Partnerships.* Available at www.teachernet.gov.uk/publications

Department for Children, Schools and Families and the Department of Health (2008a) *Children and Young People in Mind: The Final Report of the National CAMHS Review.* Nottingham: DCSF Publications.

Department for Children, Schools and Families and the Department of Health (2008b) *The Bercow Report: A Review of Services for Children and Young People (0–19) with Speech, Language and Communication Needs.* Nottingham: DCSF Publications.

Department for Children, Schools and Families and the Department of Health (2010) *Keeping Children and Young People in Mind: The Government's Full Response to the Independent Review of CAMHS*. Nottingham: DCSF Publications.

Department for Children, Schools and Families (2009a) *Learning Behaviour: Lessons Learned*. Nottingham: DCSF Publications.

Department for Children, Schools and Families (2009b) *The Children's Plan Two Years On: A Progress Report*. Available at www.teachernet.gov.uk/publications

Department for Children, Schools and Families (2009c) *Your Child, Your Schools, Our Future: Building a 21st Century School System*. Available at www.dcsf.gov.gov.uk/21stcenturyschoolssystem

Department for Children, Schools and Families (2009d) *United Nations Convention on the Rights of the Child: Priorities for Action*. Nottingham: DfES Publications.

Department for Children, Schools and Families (2009e) Apprenticeships, Skills, Children and Learning Act. The Stationery Office: Norwich.

Department for Children, Schools and Families (2009f) *Co-operative Schools – Making a Difference*. Nottingham: DCSF Publications.

Department for Children, Schools and Families (2009g) *Identifying and Teaching Children and Young People with Dyslexia and Literacy Difficulties*. Nottingham: DCSF Publications.

Department for Children, Schools and Families (2009h) *The Lamb Inquiry: Special Educational Needs and Parental Confidence*. Available at www.dcsf.gov.uk/lambinquiry

Department for Children, Schools and Families (2009i) *Review of SEN and Disability Information (April '09)*. Available at www.dcsf.gov.uk/lambinquiry

Department for Children, Schools and Families (2009j) *Inspection, Accountability and School Improvement (August '09)*. Available at www.dcsf.gov.uk/lambinquiry

Department for Children, Schools and Families (2009k) *Quality and Clarity of Statements (August '09)*. Available at www.dcsf.gov.uk/lambinquiry

Department for Children, Schools and Families (2009l) *Statutory Guidance for Local Authorities and Schools on Information Passports, Personal Learning Plans and the Core Entitlement for all Pupils in Pupil Referral Units and other Alternative Provision*. Draft for consultation 10.12.09. Available at www.teachernet.gov.uk/publications

Department for Children, Schools and Families (2010a) *Children, Schools and Families Bill*. Available at www.publications.parliament.uk

Department for Children, Schools and Families (2010b) *Salt Review – Independent Review of Teacher Supply for Pupils with Severe, Profound and Multiple Learning Difficulties (SLD and PMLD)*. Nottingham: DCSF Publications.

Department for Education and Employment (1994) *Code of Practice on the Identification and Assessment of Special Educational Needs*. London: HMSO.

Department for Education and Science (1970) *Education (Handicapped) Children Act*. London: HMSO.

Department for Education and Science (1981) *Education Act*. London: HMSO.

Department for Education and Skills (1988) *Education Reform Act*. Nottingham: DfES Publications.

Department for Education and Skills (2001a) *SEN and Disability Act.* Nottingham: DfES Publications.

Department for Education and Skills (2001b) *Special Educational Needs Code of Practice.* Nottingham: DfES Publications.

Department for Education and Skills (2003) *Every Child Matters.* London: The Stationery Office.

Department for Education and Skills (2004a) *The Children Act.* Norwich: HMSO.

Department for Education and Skills (2004b) *Removing Barriers to Achievement: The Government's SEN Strategy.* Nottingham: DfES Publications.

Department for Education and Skills (2005a) *Higher Standards, Better Schools for All.* Nottingham: DfES Publications.

Department for Education and Skills (2005b) *Learning Behaviour: The Report of The Practitioners' Group on School Behaviour and Discipline.* Nottingham: DfES Publications.

Department for Education and Skills (2005c) *Harnessing Technology: Transforming Learning and Children's Services.* Nottingham: DfES Publications.

Department for Education and Skills (2005d) *Personalising Learning: Building a New Relationship with Schools.* Speech by David Miliband, Minister of State for School Standards, North of England Conference, Belfast 08.01.04. Available at www.publications.teachernet.gov.uk

Department for Education and Skills (2006a) *The Education and Inspections Act.* Norwich: HMSO.

Department for Education and Skills (2006b) *2020 Vision: Report of the Teaching and Learning in 2020 Review Group.* Nottingham: DfES Publications.

Dittrich, W.H. and Tutt, R. (2008) *Educating Children with Complex Conditions: Understanding Overlapping and Co-existing Developmental Disorders.* London: Sage.

Gardner, H. (2000) *Intelligence Reframed: Multiple Intelligences for the 21st Century.* New York: Basic Books.

Hill, R. (2006) *Leadership that Lasts: Sustainable School Leadership in the 21st Century.* Leicester: Association of School and College Leaders.

Hill, R. (2008) *Achieving More Together: Adding Value Through Partnership.* Leicester: Association of School and College Leaders.

House of Commons Education and Skills Committee (2007) *Special Educational Needs: Assessment and Funding.* Norwich: The Stationery Office.

Knight, S. (2009) *Forest Schools and Outdoor Learning in the Early Years.* London: Sage.

Leadbetter, C. (2008) *What's Next? 21 Ideas for 21st Century Learning.* London: The Innovation Unit.

Lindsay, G. and Peacey, N. (2009) *Lamb Inquiry: Local Authorities' Learning from the Eight Projects.* Available at www.dcsf.gov.uk/lambinquiry

Nind, M. and Hewett, D. (2001) *A Practical Guide to Intensive Interaction.* Kidderminster: BILD Publications.

Office of the First Minister and Deputy First Minister (2006) *Our Children and Young People – Our Pledge: A Ten Year Strategy for Children and Young People in Northern Ireland.* Belfast: Children and Young People's Unit.

Ofsted (2009) *Virtual Learning Environments: An Evaluation of Their Development in a Sample of Educational Settings*. Available at www.ofsted.gov.uk

Scottish Government (2006) *Getting it Right for Every Child*. Available from www.scotland.gov.uk

Skinner, B.F. (1953) *Science and Human Behavior*. New York: Macmillan.

Smith, A. (2009) *Learning to Learn in Practice: The L2 Approach*. Carmarthen: Crown House.

Todd, L. (2007) *Partnerships for Inclusive Education*. London: Routledge.

Tutt, R. (2007) *Every Child Included*. London: Paul Chapman Publishing.

UNICEF (2007) *Little Book of Children's Rights and Responsibilities*. Available free from the UNICEF helpline at www.unicef.org.uk

Warnock, M. (1978) *Report of the Committee of Enquiry into the Education of Handicapped Children and Young People*. London: HMSO.

Index

INCLUSIVE PLAY

Practical Strategies for Children from Birth to Eight

Second Edition

Theresa Casey *President of the International Play Association*

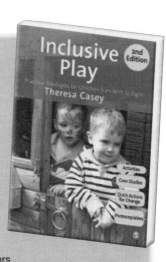

'Written from the author's deep commitment to young children's play, this second edition is straightforward and enthusiastically written and packed with good advice and activities to both enhance and challenge current play practices and adults' thinking. It's a great combination of initial theoretical justification followed by many good examples of play situations to which practitioners can relate' - *Professor Emeritus Janet Moyles, Early Years & Play Consultant*

This extremely practical and child-focused book gives you the tools you need to make sure all the children in your care are included and involved in the play opportunities of your setting.

Inside the second edition, new content includes:

- consideration of the early years curricula across the whole of the UK
- a new chapter on risk and challenge in play- new case studies
- international perspectives
- full coverage of the Birth to Eight age range
- consideration of inclusive play from a children's rights perspective.

CONTENTS

Understanding Inclusive Play \ Play Environments that Support, Intrigue, Challenge and Inspire \ Enabling Inclusive Play Opportunities- The Role of Adults \ Creative Input, Playful Opportunities \ Risk, Challenge and Uncertainty in Inclusive Settings \ Working Together \ Managing for Inclusive Play

 April 2010 • 136 pages
Cloth (978-1-84920-123-0)
Paper (978-1-84920-124-7)

ALSO FROM SAGE

I CAN'T DO THAT!

My Social Stories to Help with Communication, Self-Care and Personal Skills

Second Edition

John Ling

'This continues to be a very helpful resource for parents and professionals working with children with a range of social communication difficulties. Particularly useful, besides the examples of social stories provided, are the additional features, including how to use them, how to write your own and the further reading lists' - *Sarah Worth, Specialist Speech and Language Therapist, Cheshire Autism Support and Development Team*

Are you teaching or supporting students with special educational needs (SEN) who are struggling with social rules and conventions? This book introduces you to the concept of social stories which are a positive and practical way to help children with these difficulties.

The new edition of this book has over 90 examples of social stories, including over 30 new stories and also contains a new section on:

- why social stories are important
- how to use them in your setting
- how to write your own social stories.

Suitable for use with children of any age, the book includes examples for those children with language delays, communication difficulties, difficult behaviour, antisocial behaviour as well as those with autism. Broken down into 8 sections it is easy to find an example suitable for the situation you are facing so you can work together with the child to create their personal story.

CONTENTS

How to use this book \ How to use a social story \ Writing your own stories \ Section 1: Me and my body \ Section 2: Home routines \ Section 3: Eating habits \ Section 4: My feelings \ Section 5: Social skills \ Section 6: Play and friendship \ Section 7: School routines \ Section 8: School work

LUCKY DUCK BOOKS

September 2010 • 120 pages
Paper (978-0-85702-044-4)

ALSO FROM SAGE

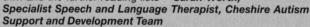

SPECIAL NEEDS AND EARLY YEARS

A Practitioner Guide

Third Edition

Kate Wall *University of Chichester*

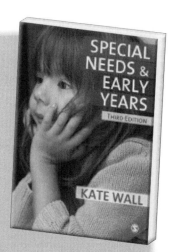

'This wide-ranging and theoretically grounded update of a key text is extremely user-friendly for both academics and students wishing to gain an insight into the impact of Special Needs within the widening early years workforce' - *Julia Druce, Senior Lecturer and Pathway Leader for Early Years, Playwork and Education, Anglia Ruskin University*

In the third edition of this respected and influential textbook, Kate Wall blends theory and practice to provide a detailed analysis of provision for young children with additional needs.

New to this edition are:

- up-to-date information on all the relevant policies and legislation, including the Early Years Foundation Stage (EYFS), Every Child Matters (ECM) and the training guidelines for new SENCOs
- a timeline showing the development of policies and legislation in the field
- learning objectives at the beginning of chapters
- points for reflection within chapters, to aid independent study and facilitate critical thinking
- new case studies, which cover the Birth to 8 age range
- new content on the role of fathers, pupil voice and listening to children, taking an holistic view of the child, and current issues around diversity and inclusion.

CONTENTS

Relevant legislation and policy \ Families of Children with Special Needs \ Partnerships with Parents \ Considering the Child Holistically \ Observation and Assessment \ Programmes of Intervention \ Interagency Working \ Issues of Diversity and Inclusion \ Issues for Consideration

December 2010 • 256 pages
Cloth (978-1-84920-132-2)
Paper (978-1-84920-133-9)

ALSO FROM SAGE

AUTISM AND EARLY YEARS PRACTICE

Second Edition

Kate Wall *University of Chichester*

'This is a leading book in the field of autism and an essential read for all early years students, practitioners and parents' - *Early Years Educator*

This new edition of the leading book in autism and early years practice continues to provide excellent guidance for all early years students and practitioners on how to work with young children who have autism or who appear on the autistic spectrum.

Kate Wall's wise words will resonate with all, as she sets out clear and realistic suggestions for ways to include young children with autism in mainstream settings, supporting her advice with case studies based on her own experience as a practitioner. Each chapter also looks at key issues and offers suggestions for discussion.

Highlights of the new edition include:

- coverage of the latest developments in research
- reference to current early years legislation, including the Early Years Foundation Stage (EYFS)
- new case studies, covering the full 0 to 8 age range
- more suggestions for discussion
- updated key texts for further reading.

CONTENTS

Tricia David Foreward \ Definitions of autism, common features and relevant legislation \ Families of children with autism \ Issues of diagnosis and assessment \ Understanding the world of the child with autism \ Programmes of intervention \ Providing for young children with autism \ Mainstream or special? Issues of inclusion \ Key issues and suggestions for the future

IC

2009 • 176 pages
Cloth (978-1-84787-507-5)
Paper (978-1-84787-508-2)

ALSO FROM SAGE